DATE DUE

Seal of the State of Illinois

CHRONOLOGY AND DOCUMENTARY HANDBOOK OF THE STATE OF ILLINOIS

ROBERT I. VEXLER

State Editor

WILLIAM F. SWINDLER

Series Editor

1978 OCEANA PUBLICATIONS, INC./Dobbs Ferry, New York

Library of Congress Cataloging in Publication Data

Main entry under title:

Chronology and documentary handbook of the State of
    Illinois.

    (Chronologies and documentary handbooks of the States;
v. 13)
    Bibliography: p.
    Includes index.
    SUMMARY: A chronology of historical events from
1659-1977, a biographical outline of politicians and personalities,
and selected documents.
    1. Illinois — History — Chronology. 2. Illinois —
Biography. 3. Illinois — History — Sources. [1. Illinois —
History] I. Vexler, Robert I. II. Series.
F541.C55   977.3   78-6661
ISBN 0-379-16138-9

977.3
√

Manufactured in the United States of America

TABLE OF CONTENTS

ACKNOWLEDGMENT

Special recognition should be accorded Melvin Hecker, whose research has made a valuable contribution to this volume.

Thanks to my wife, Francine, in appreciation of her help in the preparation of this work.

Thanks also to my children, David and Melissa, without whose patience and understanding I would have been unable to devote the considerable time necessary for completing the state chronology series.

Robert I. Vexler

INTRODUCTION

This projected series of <u>Chronologies and Documentary Handbooks of the States</u> will ultimately comprise fifty separate volumes - one for each of the states of the Union. Each volume is intended to provide a concise ready reference of basic data on the state, and to serve as a starting point for more extended study as the individual user may require. Hopefully, it will be a guidebook for a better informed citizenry - students, civic and service organizations, professional and business personnel, and others.

The editorial plan for the <u>Handbook</u> series falls into six divisions: (1) a chronology of selected events in the history of the state; (2) a short biographical directory of the principal public officials, e.g., governors, Senators and Representatives; (3) a short biographical directory of prominent personalities of the state (for most states); (4) the first state constitution; (5) the text of some representative documents illustrating main currents in the political, economic, social or cultural history of the state; and (6) a selected bibliography for those seeking further or more detailed information. Most of the data found in the present volume, in fact, have been taken from one or another of these references.

The current constitutions of all fifty states, as well as the federal Constitution, are regularly kept up to date in the definitive collection maintained by the Legislative Drafting Research Fund of Columbia University and published by the publisher of the present series of <u>Handbooks</u>. These texts are available in most major libraries under the title, <u>Constitutions of the United States: National and State</u>, in two volumes, with a companion volume, the <u>Index Digest of State Constitutions</u>.

Finally, the complete collection of documents illustrative of the constitutional development of each state, from colonial or territorial status up to the current constitution as found in the Columbia University collection, is being prepared for publication in a multi-volume series by the present series editor. Whereas the present series of <u>Handbooks</u> is intended for a wide range of interested citizens, the series of annotated constitutional materials in the volumes of <u>Sources and Documents of U. S. Constitutions</u> is primarily for the specialist in government, history or law. This is not to suggest that the general citizenry may not profit equally from referring to these materials; rather, it points up the separate purpose of the <u>Handbooks</u>, which is to guide the user to these and other sources of authoritative information with which he may systematically enrich his knowledge of this state and its place in the American Union.

William F. Swindler
Series Editor

Robert I. Vexler
Series Associate Editor

State Sovereignty - National Union

State Motto

CHRONOLOGY

1659   Pierre Radisson and Medard Chouart des Gro-
        seilliers reached the Upper Mississippi
        River.

1673   Louis Joliet and the Jesuit Priest Jacques
        Marquette explored part of the region known
        as the Illinois County for France.

1675   Jacques Marquette founded a mission at Kas-
        kaskia, an Indian town, near the site of
        the present Utica, Illinois.

1679   French explorer Robert Cavalier, Sieur de la
        Salle ascended the St. Joseph River, crossed
        over to the Kanakee River, travelling down
        it to the Illinois.

1680   Robert Cavalier, Sieur de la Salle, con-
        structed Fort Crevecoeur on the Lake of
        Peoria in the midst of the Illinois tribes.

1681   Winter. Robert Cavalier, Sieur de la Salle
        returned to the Illinois area.

1682   De La Salle reached the mouth of the Illinois
        River.

1690   Henri de Tonty and La Forest were granted
        all Robert de La Salle's rights in the Illi-
        nois.

1699   The Seminary for Foreign Missions established
        a mission to the Tamaroa Indians at Cahokia
        in the American Bottom.

        The Sieur d'Iberville founded Biloxi.

        French settlers founded the first permanent
        town at Cahokia near what is present-day
        East St. Louis.

1712   The Illinois River became the northern
        boundary of the French province of Louisiana.

1720   About this year a manuscript dictionary of
        the Illinois Indians' language along with a
        catechism and prayers was issued. It was
        thought to be the work of Father LeBoulanger.

        Philippe Renault came to the Illinois region
        in search of mines.

        Construction of Fort de Chartres was begun.

It was rebuilt as the Louisbourg of the West
in 1753.

Kaskaskia, near the mouth of the Kaskaskia
River, was established.

Ouiatenon, near the present town of Lafayette, Indiana, was founded.

1721   The French government established the seventh
        civil and military district of its province
        of Louisiana, naming it Illinois. This re-
        gion included more than one-half of the pre-
        sent state of Illinois and the country be-
        tween the Mississippi River and the Rocky
        Mountains.

1723   The region surrounding the Wabash River was
        formed into a separate district.

1731   Vincennes was founded.

1733   Pierre Dartaguiette was appointed the com-
        mandant of Illinois and served until 1736.

1757   Fort Massac was constructed opposite the
        mouth of the Tennessee River.

1759   Fort Gage was erected at Kaskaskia.

1763   As a result of the Treaty of Paris Great
        Britain received from France the territory
        between the Ohio and the Mississippi Rivers
        which included Illinois. The English were
        not able to take over the area until 1765
        because of Pontiac's conspiracy, the great
        Indian uprising.

1765   Summer. Sir William Johnson had completed
        a peaceful settlement and pacification of
        the Indians in the Wabash country.

1771   Residents of the Illinois region met at
        Kaskaskia where they requested a form of
        self-government similar to that of Connecti-
        cut. General Thomas Gage rejected the peti-
        tion. The Secretary of State for the Plan-
        tations and President of the Board of Trade
        Thomas Legge, the Earl of Dartmouth, formu-
        lated a plan of government in which all
        officials were to be appointed by the Crown.

1772   Fort de Chartres was demolished.

1773   William Murray purchased most of Southern
            Illinois for an Illinois land company. This
            was based on the option of the firm of Gratz
            and Company.

1774   The Quebec Act was passed annexing Illinois
            to the province of Quebec.

1778   George Rogers Clark captured Kaskaskia and
            Cahokia during the American Revolutionary
            War.

            The Virginia House of Delegates extended
            the civil jurisdiction of Virginia to the
            territory of the northwest. Captain John
            Todd of Kentucky was named governor of the
            entire territory north of the Ohio River.
            It was organized as "The County of Illinois."

1779   The first Americans made their permanent
            homes in the Illinois region.

1780   The English sent an expedition of troops from
            Detroit and Mackinac to reconquer the Illi-
            nois territory.

1783   September 30. By the Peace Treaty of 1783
            between Great Britain and the United States
            which ended the Revolutionary War the United
            States received title to Illinois and the
            Northwest.

1787   By the Northwest Ordinance of 1787 the terri-
            tory west of the Alleghenies was organized
            into the Northwest Territory. Various states
            had given up their claims to the area.

1790   April 27. St. Clair County was created with
            Belleville as its county seat. It was named
            in honor of Governor Arthur St. Clair, first
            governor of the Northwest Territory from
            1788 to 1802.

1793   Rev. Joseph Lillard, the first Methodist
            preacher, appeared.

1795   October 5. The southern part of St. Clair
            County was organized as Randolph County with
            its seat at Chester. It was named for Edmund
            Jennings Randolph, Governor of Virginia, first
            Attorney General in the Cabinet of President
            George Washington as well as Secretary of
            State.

1796   The first Baptist Church was established at
            New Design.

1800   The Illinois Country was included in Indiana
            Territory.

1804   The United States Congress established a
            land office at Kaskaskia to examine existing
            claims and to eliminate all conflict with
            future grants of land.

1809   February 9. Congress set off Illinois Terri-
            tory: the western part of Indiana from Vin-
            cennes north to Canada. This territory
            included the present state of Illinois and
            most of Wisconsin except the northern part
            of the Green Bay peninsula as well as a
            large portion of Michigan and all of Minne-
            sota east of the Mississippi River.

            Ninian Edwards was appointed Territorial Gov-
            ernor and continued in office until 1818.

1810   Population: 12,282

1812   August 15-16. Great Britain's Indian allies
            killed the United States troops and settlers
            at Fort Dearborn at the site of present-
            day Chicago. This occurred during the War
            of 1812.

            September 14. The following counties were
            established: Gallatin with its county seat
            at Shawneetown, Johnson with its seat at
            Vienna, and Madison with its county seat at
            Edwardsville. Gallatin County was named for
            Abraham Alfonse Albert Gallatin, Secretary
            of Treasury in the Cabinet of President
            Thomas Jefferson; Johnson for Richard Mentor
            Johnson, Representative from Kentucky
            and later to be Vice President under Martin
            Van Buren; and Madison for James Madison,
            fourth President of the United States.

            New land offices were established at Shawnee-
            town and Edwardsville for the sale of public
            lands.

            Congress gave permission for the selection
            of a representative territorial assembly.
            A territorial constitution was adopted, and
            the Territorial delegate to Congress was
            elected directly by the people.

The Territory of Illinois voted almost unanimously to proceed to the second grade of territorial government.

1814   November 28. Edwards County was created with its seat at Albion. It was named for Ninian Edwards, first territorial governor and third governor of Illinois.

The first paper in Illinois was published at Kaskaskia, the <u>Illinois Herald</u>.

1816   January 6. Monroe County with its county seat at Waterloo was established. It was named for James Monroe, former member of the Continental Congress and Secretary of State in the Cabinet of President James Madison. Monroe was soon to be elected fifth President of the United States.

January 10. Jackson and Pope Counties were created. Jackson with its county seat at Murphysboro was named for Andrew Jackson, Representative from Tennessee, major general in the United States Army during the War of 1812 and leader of the victory at New Orleans in 1815. He was later to be the seventh President of the United States. Pope with its seat at Golconda was named for Nathaniel Pope, first territorial Secretary of Illinois Territory and then Congressional Delegate from Illinois.

December 31. Crawford County was established with its county seat at Robinson. It was named for William Harris Crawford, Secretary of War and then Secretary of the Treasury in the Cabinet of President James Madison.

1817   January 4. Bond County was established with its county seat at Greenville. It was named for Shadrach Bond who was to become the first governor of Illinois in 1818.

1818   January 2. The following counties were established: Franklin with its county seat at Benton; Union with its county seat at Jonesboro; and Washington with its county seat at Nashville. Franklin was named for Benjamin Franklin who served in the Continental Congress, signed the Declaration of Independence, served as diplomat to France and attended the Constitutional Convention. Washington

County was named for George Washington, first President of the United States.

August 3. The constitutional convention opened. It completed its work on August 26. The Constitution was then adopted by the citizens.

December 3. Illinois was admitted as the 21st state.

Shadrach Bond became governor of the state and served until 1822.

Peter Kimmel began publishing the _Illinois Emigrant_.

1819   March 4. Alexander County was established with its county seat at Cairo. It was named for William M. Alexander one of the early Illinois settlers and eventually a member of the Illinois house of representatives.

March 22. Clark County was established with its county seat at Marshall. It was named for George Rogers Clark, brigadier general in the Continental Army.

March 26. Jefferson and Wayne Counties were created. Jefferson with its county seat at Mount Vernon was named for Thomas Jefferson, 3rd President of the United States. Wayne with its county seat at Fairfield was named for Anthony Wayne, major general and general-in-chief of the United States Army and Representative from Georgia.

The state legislature chartered a state bank with authorization to do business on the credit of the state.

1820   Population: 55,211

1821   January 16. Lawrence County was established with its county seat at Lawrenceville. It was named for James Lawrence, United States naval commander.

January 20. Green County was created with Carrollton as its county seat. It was named for Nathaniel Greene who served in the Continental Army.

January 30. Sangamon County was established
with Springfield as its county seat.

January 31. Pike County was established with
Pittsfield as its county seat. It was named
for Zebulon Montgomery Pike who discovered
Pike's Peak.

February 8. Hamilton County was created with
McLeansboro as the county seat. It was named
for Alexander Hamilton, Secretary of the
Treasury in the Cabinet of President George
Washington.

February 12. Montgomery County was established with its county seat at Hillsboro.
It was named for Richard Montgomery who had
been a brigadier general in the Continental
Army and was killed leading an assault
against Quebec on December 31, 1775.

February 14. Fayette County was created with
its county seat at Vandalia. It was named
for the Marquis de Lafayette who aided the
American struggle for independence and was
commissioned a major general in the Continental Army.

1822   Edward Coles, Democrat, became governor and
          served until 1826.

1823   January 3. Edgar County was established
          with Paris as its county seat. It was named
          for John Edgar who had been an early mer-
          chant and a politician.

          January 24. Marion County was established
          with its county seat at Salem. It was named
          for Francis Marion who had served in the
          Revolutionary War and won the battle of Eutaw
          Springs.

          January 28. Fulton County was created with
          its county seat at Lewiston. It was named
          for Robert Fulton the inventor who developed
          the steam engine and built the Clermont, a
          steamboat, which sailed up the Hudson River
          in 1807.

          January 31. Morgan County was established
          with its county seat at Jacksonville. It was
          named for Daniel Morgan who served in the
          Revolutionary War and helped to suppress the

Whiskey Rebellion in Pennsylvania.

The legislature submitted a resolution to the people for a constitutional convention to amend the constitution for the unexpressed aim of legalizing slavery.

1824   December 23. Clay County was established with its county seat at Louisville. It was named for Henry Clay, Representative and Senator from Kentucky. He was later Secretary of State in the Cabinet of President John Quincy Adams.

December 27. Wabash County was created with Mt. Carmel as its county seat. Clinton County was also established with Carlyle as its county seat. It was named for De Witt Clinton, governor of New York and Senator from New York.

The citizens of the state rejected the proposal for calling a constitutional convention which might have introduced slavery into Illinois.

1825   January 10. Calhoun County with its county seat at Hardin was created. It was named for John Caldwell Calhoun, Representative and Senator from South Carolina, Vice President of the United States under Presidents John Quincy Adams and Andrew Jackson and Secretary of State in the Cabinet of President John Tyler.

January 13. The following counties were established: Adams with its county seat at Quincy; Hancock with its county seat at Carthage; Henry with its county seat at Cambridge; Knox with its county seat at Galesburg; Mercer with its county seat at Alcedo; Peoria with its county seat at Peroia; Putnam with its county seat at Hennepin; and Schuyler with its county seat at Rushville. Adams was named for John Quincy Adams, 6th President of the United States; Hancock, for John Hancock, governor of Massachusetts and first signer of the Declaration of Independence; Henry, for Patrick Henry, governor of Virginia and member of the Continental Congress; Knox, for Henry Knox, brigadier general in the Continental Army and Secretary of War in the Cabinet of President George

Washington; Mercer, for Hugh Mercer, a
physician who served in the Revolutionary
War and was wounded at the battle of Princeton on January 3, 1777 and died of these
wounds on January 12; Peoria, for the Peoria
Indian tribe; Putnam, for Israel Putnam who
served in the army during the French and
Indian War, Pontiac's War and the Revolutionary War; and Schuyler, for Philip John
Schuyler, major general in the Continental
Army and Senator from New York.

1826   January 18. Vermilion County was established
with Danville as its county seat.

January 25. McDonough County was created
with its county seat at Macomb. It was named
for Thomas McDonough who served in the United
States Navy, fighting against the Tripoli
Pirates and against the British during the
War of 1812.

Ninian Edwards, Democrat, became governor.
He served until 1830.

1827   January 29. Perry County was established
with Pinckneyville as its county seat. It
was named for Commodore Oliver Hazard Perry,
who constructed and commanded a fleet on
Lake Erie which defeated the British fleet.

January 31. Tazewell County was established
with its county seat at Pelein. It was
named for Littleton Waller Tazewell, Representative and Senator from Virginia as well
as governor of the state.

February 17. Jo Daviess County was created
with Galena as its county seat. It was named
for Joseph Hamilton Daviess, the United
States District Attorney who prosecuted Aaron
Burr for treason in 1807. He was killed
at the Battle of Tippecanoe on November 7,
1811.

The Winnebago War broke out.

1829   Macoupin County was established with its
county seat at Carlinville.

January 19. Macon County was established
with Decatur as county seat. It was named
for Nathaniel Macon, Representative and

Senator from North Carolina and Speaker of
the House of Representatives from 1801 to
1807.

Illinois College was founded at Jacksonville.

1830   Population: 157,445.

December 6. John Reynolds, National Republican became governor and served until his
resignation on November 17, 1834.

December 25. McLean County was created with
Bloomington as county seat. It was named for
John McClean, Representative and Senator from
Illinois.

December 26. Coles County was established
with its county seat at Charleston. It was
named for Edward Coles, governor of Illinois.

Chicago was laid out at the site of Fort
Dearborn.

1831   January 15. Cook and La Salle Counties
were established. Cook with its county seat
at Chicago was named for Daniel Pope Cook,
attorney general of Illinois and Representative from Illinois. La Salle with its seat
at Ottawa was named for Robert Cavalier de
la Salle, the French explorer who sailed
down the Mississippi River to the Gulf of
Mexico and claimed the entire territory for
the French king.

February 9. Rock Island Couty was established with its county seat at Rock Island.

February 15. Effingham and Jasper Counties
were created. Effingham's county seat was
located at Effingham. Jasper with its county
seat at Newton was named for William Jasper
who served in the Revolutionary war.

Governor John Reynolds called out the militia
to speed up the withdrawal of the Sauk and
Fox Indians from northern Illinois.

1832   April 6. Chief Black Hawk of the Sauk Indian
tribe began a war against the United States
with an attack on Rock River, Illinois. He
was surrendered to the government by the
Winnebago Indians on August 27, 1832.

1833   February 20. Champaign County was established
                with Urbana as its county seat.

                February 26. Iroquois County with its county
                seat at Wataka was established. It was named
                for the Iroquois Indian tribe.

                John Deere, a blacksmith at Grand Detour
                developed the first steel plow.

1834   November 17. Lieutenant Governor William L.
                D. Ewing, Democrat became governor upon the
                resignation of Governor John Reynolds.
                Ewing served until December 3, 1834.

                December 3. Joseph Duncan, Whig, became
                governor and served until December 7, 1838.

1835   February 9. Illinois College was chartered
                at Jacksonville, Illinois. The first degrees
                were awarded in 1835.

                A second state bank was chartered. It sus-
                pended payment in 1837, and the legislature
                provided for its liquidation in 1843.

1836   January 12. Will County was created with
                Joliet as the county seat. It was named for
                Conrad Will, a member of the Illinois general
                assembly.

                January 16. The following counties were es-
                tablished: Kane with its county seat at Ge-
                neva; McHenry with its county seat at Wood-
                stock; Ogle with its county seat at Oregon;
                Whiteside with its county seat at Morrison;
                and Winnebago with its county seat at Rock-
                ford. Kane was named for Elisha Kent Kane,
                Senator from Illinois; Will for Conrad Will,
                a member of the Illinois general assembly;
                McHenry for William McHenry who served in
                the War of 1812 and the Black Hawk War in
                1832; Ogle for Joseph Ogle, a member of the
                Illinois militia; Whiteside for Samuel White-
                side, who served in the War of 1812 and the
                Black Hawk War and was a member of the Illi-
                nois assembly.

                The state granted a loan to a company to con-
                struct the Illinois and Michigan canal.

1837   Shelby County was created with the county
                seat at Shelbyville, It was named for Isaac

Shelby who served in the Revolutionary War
and the War of 1812 and was governor of Kentucky.

February 15. Knox College was chartered as
Knox Manual Labor College at Galesburg, Illinois. It granted its first degrees in 1846
and became Knox College in 1857.

February 27. Livingston County with its
county seat at Pontiac was created. It was
named for Edward Livingston, a member of
General Andrew Jackson's staff at the battle
of New Orleans and was later Secretary of
State in President Jackson's cabinet.

February 28. Bureau County was established
with its county seat at Princeton. It was
named for Pierre de Buero, a French fur
trader.

March 3. Cass County was created with Virginia as its county seat. It was named for
Lewis Cass, governor of Michigan territory,
army officer, Secretary of War in the Cabinet of President Andrew Jackson and later
Secretary of State in President James Buchanan's cabinet.

March 4. The following counties were established: Boone, De Kalb, and Stephenson.
Boone with its county seat at Belvidere was
named for Daniel Boone; De Kalb with its seat
at Sycamore was named for Johann De Kalb,
a Frenchman who served in the Continental
Army during the Revolution as a major general; and Stephenson with its seat at Freeport
was named for Benjamin Stephenson, veteran
of the War of 1812 and Delegate from the
Illinois Territory.

McKendree College was founded at Lebanon.

The state government appropriated $10,000,000
for internal improvements including the construction of railroads. Because the state's
credit declined and a heavy debt incurred
the policy was abandoned.

1838   December 7. Thomas Carlin, Democrat, became governor and served until December 8,
1842

1839   January 19. Marshall County was established
              with Lacon as county seat. It was named for
              John Marshall, Secretary of State in the ca-
              binet of President John Adams and Chief
              Justice of the United States Supreme Court.

              February 1. Brown County was created with
              Mount Sterling as the county seat. It was
              named for Jacob Brown who served in the
              army during the War of 1812.

              February 9. Du Page County was established
              with Wheaton as its county seat, It was named
              for Du Page an Indian.

              February 15. Christian, Logan and Menard
              Counties were created. Christian with its
              county seat at Taylorville was originally
              named Dane County and was changed to Christian
              on February 1, 1840. Logan County with its
              seat at Lincoln was named for Dr. John Lo-
              gan. and Menard with its seat at Petersburg
              for Pierre Menard, the first presiding offi-
              cer of the Illinois territorial legislature.

              February 16. Scott County was established
              with its county seat at Winchester. It was
              named for Scott County, Kentucky.

              February 22. Carroll County with Mount Car-
              roll as its county seat was created. It was
              named for Charles Carroll, a member of the
              Continental Congress and a Senator form Mary-
              land as well as the last surviving signer
              of the Declaration of Independence.

              February 27. Lee County was established with
              its county seat at Dixon. It was named for
              named for Richard Henry Lee, a signer of the
              Declaration of Independence and a Senator from
              Virginia.

              February 28. Jersey and Williamson Counties
              were created. Jersey with its county seat at
              Jerseyville was named for New Jersey. Wil-
              liamson with Marion as its seat was named for
              Williamson County, Tennessee, which had been
              named for Hugh Williamson.

              March 1. Dewitt and Lake Counties were estab-
              lished. Dewitt with its county seat at
              Clinton was named for De Witt Clinton, gover-
              nor of New York. Lake County, a descriptive

term, had its county seat at Waukegan.

March 2. Hardin and Stark Counties were created. Hardin with its county seat at Elizabeth town was named for Hardin County, Kentucky. Stark with Toulon as its county seat
was named for John Stark who fought in the
French and Indian and the Revolutionary Wars.

1840   Population: 476,183.

The Mormons came to Navoo in Hancock County
on the Mississippi River for safety and
security reasons.

1841   January 20. Henderson and Mason Counties
were created. Henderson with its county seat
at Oquawka was named for Richard Henderson.
Mason with its county seat at Havana was
named for Mason County, Kentucky.

January 27. Platt County with Monticello
as the county seat was established. It was
named for Benjamin Platt, an attorney general of Illinois territory.

February 17. Grundy County was created with
Morris as its county seat. It was named for
Felix Grundy, Attorney General in the Cabinet
of President Martin Van Buren.

February 19. Kendall County was established
with its county seat at Yorkville. It was
named for Amos Kendall, Postmaster General
in the Cabinets of Presidents Andrew Jackson
and Martin Van Buren.

February 24. Richland County with its seat
at Olney was created, named for Richland
County, Ohio.

February 27. Woodford County was established
with Eureka as its county seat.

1842   December 8. Thomas Ford, Democrat, became
governor. He served in this office until
December 9, 1846.

1843   February 8. Massac County with its county
seat at Metropolis was created. It was named
for Fort Massac.

February 16. Moultrie County was established

with Sullivan as its county seat. It was named for William Moultrie who was governor of South Carolina.

March 2. Cumberland County with its county seat at Toledo was created. It was named for William Augustus, Duke of Cumberland, second son of King George II and Queen Caroline.

March 3. Pulaski County was established with Mound City as its county seat. It was named for Casimir Pulaski, a Polish nobleman who had aided the Americans in their struggle for independence.

1844 June 27. Joseph Smith, the founder of Mormonism, and his brother Hiram Smith were killed by a mob in Carthage, Illinois.

1846 December 9. Augustus C. French, Democrat, became governor and served until January 10, 1853.

MacMurray College was founded at Jacksonville, and St. Xavier College at Chicago.

1847 February 25. Saline County was created with Harrisburg as its county seat.

Rockford College was founded at Rockford.

1848 The Illinois and Michigan Canal was finished. It linked the Great Lakes to the Mississippi River.

The Constitution of 1848 was adopted, abolishing slavery and prohibiting the immigration of slaves into the state.

Rosary College was founded at River Forest.

1850 Population: 851,470.

Illinois Wesleyan University was founded at Bloomington.

1851 January 28. Northwestern University was founded at Evanston, Illinois as North Western University. It combined the two terms in 1867.

Construction of the Chicago and Rock Island

Railroad was begun.

1853   January 10. Joel A. Matteson, Democrat, who had been elected in 1852, became governor.

February 11. Kankakee County was created. It was named for the Kankakee Indian tribe with its county seat at Kankakee.

February 12. Illinois Wesleyan University received its charter. It is located in Bloomington.

Monmouth College was founded at Monmouth, and Shimer College at Mount Carroll.

Barnum's Grand Colossal Museum and Menagerie toured Illinois in 1853.

1854   March 18. A mass meeting at Rockford helped to organize the Republican Party.

October 4-5. A Republican Convention was held at Springfield.

October 16. Abraham Lincoln spoke at Peoria, condemning slavery but denying that the Kansas-Nebraska act was part of a slaveholders' conspiracy.

The Chicago and Rock Island Railroad was completed.

1855   February 6. Eureka College was founded, granting its first degrees in 1860.

1856   The Liberty and Free Soil Parties along with those Democrats opposed to the Kansas-Nebraska Act and some Whigs formally organized the Republican Party.

The Chicago Historical Society was founded.

1857   January 12. William H. Bissell, Republican, who had been elected in 1856, became governor. He served in this office until his death on March 18, 1860.

Lake Forest College at Lake Forest, Blackburn College at Carlinville and Illinois State University at Normal were founded.

The first Chicago-St. Louis sleeping car
train was put into operation.

1858   August 21.   The first of seven debates be-
            tween Abraham Lincoln and Stephen A. Douglas
            took place as part of the campaign for Sena-
            tor.

1859   February 8.   Douglas County was created with
            its county seat at Tuscola.   It was named
            for Stephen Arnold Douglas, Representative
            and Senator from Illinois.

            February 19.   Ford County was established
            with Paxton as its county seat.   It was named
            for Thomas Ford, eighth governor of Illinois.

1860   Population: 1,711,951.

            February 15.   Wheaton College was chartered
            as the Illinois Institute in Wheaton.   It
            presented its first degrees in 1860.

            March 21.   John Wood, Republican, succeeded
            to the office of Governor and served as
            acting governor until January 14, 1861.

            May 16-18 The National Convention of the
            Republican Party met in Chicago.   Abraham
            Lincoln was nominated for President and
            Hannibal Hamlin for Vice President.

            Augustana College was founded at Rock Island
            and Quincy College at Quincy.

1861   January 14.   Richard Yates, Republican, who
            had been elected in 1860, became governor.
            He served until January 16, 1965.

            North Central College was established at
            Napierville.

            The Illinois legislature provided a war fund
            of $2,000,000 to fight the Confederacy.

1862   A constitutional convention met, but the
            constitution it developed was rejected by
            the people.

1863   July.   The Democratic Party held a mass
            meeting at Springfield where resolutions con-
            demning the suspension of the writ of habeas
            corpus, endorsing the concept of state

sovereignty and demanding a national assembly
to determine peace terms as well as requesting President Lincoln to withdraw the Emancipation Proclamation.

1864   Concordia Teachers College was founded at
River Forest.

1865   January 16. Richard J. Oglesby, Republican,
who had been elected in 1864, became gover-
nor. He served until January 11, 1869.

February 1. The state legislature ratified
the 13th Amendment to the United States
Constitution.

Elmhurst College was founded at Elmhurst.

The Union stockyards were opened in Chicago.
They eventually became the largest stockyards in the nation, serving the cattle
industry over a wide area.

1866   July 27. Orville H. Browning was appointed
Secretary of the Interior in the Cabinet of
President Andrew Johnson. He took office on
September 1, 1866.

The schools of the Art Institute of Chicago
were founded.

1867   January 15. The state legislature ratified
the 14th Amendment to the United States
Constitution.

Chicago State University was founded.

The University of Illinois was established
at Urbana as the Illinois Industrial University. The first classes met in 1868. The
present name was adopted in 1885.

The state legislature enacted the 8-hour
day but did not provide for proper enforce-
ment.

1868   May 20-21. The Republican National Convention met in Chicago. It proceeded to nomi-
nate General Ulysses S. Grant for President
and Schuyler Colfax for Vice President.

May 28. John M. Schofield was appointed
Secretary of War in the Cabinet of President

Andrew Johnson.   Schofield entered upon his
duties June 1, 1868.

William Loomis Miller bequeathed $2,000,000
for the establishment of a free public reference library in Chicago.   He had founded the
Young Men's Library Association in 1841.

The Patrons of Husbandry was organized in
Illinois.

1869   January 11.   John M. Palmer, Republican, who
            had been elected in 1869, became governor.
            He served in the office until January 13,
            1873.

            March 5.   The state legislature ratified the
            15th Amendment to the United States Consti-
            tution.

            March 5.   Elihu B. Washburne became Secretary
            of State in the Cabinet of President Ulysses
            S. Grant.

            March 11.   John A. Rawlins became Secretary
            of War in the Cabinet of President Ulysses
            S. Grant.

            June 8.   The first American patent of a
            suction-principle vacuum cleaner was awarded
            to I. W. McGafley of Chicago.

            The National Prohibition Party was founded
            in Chicago.

1870   Population: 2,549,891.

            The third state constitution was adopted.

            Loyola University was chartered as St. Ig-
            natius College at Chicago.   It changed its
            name later in the year.

1871   October 8-11.   The great Chicago fire oc-
            curred.   More than 350 people were killed;
            98,500 were left homeless as a result of
            the devastation of an area of 3½ square
            miles.   Property loss was estimated at
            $200,000,000.

            The Daily Illini began publication at the
            University of Illinois.   It became the first
            undergraduate daily paper in the United

States.

1872   Governor John W. Palmer, Senator Lyman Trumbull, Gustavus Koerner and other prominent men in the state joined the Liberal Party.

The state legislature passed a law which provided for the first regulation of mines.

The first mail order house in the United States, Montgomery Ward and Company, was opened in Chicago. Aaron Montgomery Ward established the firm whose first catalog was only a single page.

1873   January 13. Richard J. Oglesby, Republican, who had been elected in 1872, became governor. He served in office until his resignation on January 23, 1873.

January 23. Lieutenant Governor John L. Beveridge, Republican, became acting governor. He served until the end of the term on January 8, 1877.

1874   The Independent Reform Party was established. In its platform it advocated retrenchment of expenses, state regulation of railroads and a tariff for revenue only.

1875   September 10. The American Forestry Association was organized in Chicago.

1876   The Greenback Party was organized as the successor of the Independent Reform Party.

Melville E. Stone and William Dougherty began publication of the Chicago Daily News.

1877   January 8. Shelby M. Cullom, who had been elected in 1876, became governor. He was reelected in 1880 and served in office until his resignation on February 8, 1883.

In the case of Munn v. Illinois the United States Supreme Court upheld the right of a state to fix maximum rates and otherwise control business involved in the "public interest."

1880   Population: 3,077,871.

April. The National Farmers' Alliance was established at Chicago.

The *Dial* began publication in Chicago.

1881   March 5. Robert Lincoln was appointed Secretary of War in the Cabinet of President James A. Garfield. He entered upon his duties on March 11.

1883   February 16. John M. Hamilton, Republican, became acting governor upon the resignation of Shelby M. Cullom. He served in the office until the end of the term on January 30, 1885.

1885   January 30. Richard J. Oglesby, Republican, who had been elected in 1884, became governor. He served in the office until January 14, 1889.

        Governor Richard Oglesby called out the militia to suppress riots in Will and Cook Counties which had broken out as a result of the strikes of quarrymen.

1886   National College of Education was founded at Evanston.

        Governor Oglesby called out the militia to suppress riots in St. Clair and Cook Counties. The riots occurred as a result of a strike of railway employees.

1887   Illinois Benedictine College was founded at Lisle.

1888   June 25. The Republican Party held its National Convention at Chicago, Benjamin Harrison was nominated for President and Levi Morton for Vice President.

1889   January 14. Joseph W. Fifer, Republican, who had been elected in 1888, became governor. He served in office until January 10, 1893.

        Jane Addams founded Hull House in Chicago.

1890   Population: 3,826,352.

        George Williams College was founded at Downers Grove.

        The University of Chicago was established.

1891   North Park College was founded at Chicago.

            The Australian Ballot Act was passed by the
            state legislature.

1892   June 21-23. The Democratic National Con-
            vention was held in Chicago. Grover Cleve-
            land was nominated for President and Adlai
            Ewing Stevenson for Vice President.

            September. The first electric automobile,
            produced by William Morrison of Des Moines,
            Iowa, appeared in Chicago.

            Greenville College was established at Green-
            ville.

            The Illinois Institute of Technology was
            founded at Chicago.

            The Illinois state legislature passed an
            act making the anniversary of Abraham Lin-
            coln's birthday, February 12, a legal holi-
            day.

1893   January 10. John P. Altgeld, Democrat, who
            had been elected in 1892, became governor.
            He served in office until January 11, 1897.

            March 6. Walter Q. Gresham was appointed
            Secretary of State in the Cabinet of Presi-
            dent Grover Cleveland.

            August 1. The Populists and the Republicans
            formed the Bimetallic League in Chicago.

            The World's Columbian Exposition was opened
            in Chicago.

            Aurora College was founded at Aurora.

            May 11. The Pullman strike began in Chicago.
            The American Railway Union supported the
            Pullman workers by beginning a general railway
            strike on June 26. President Grover Cleveland
            put an end to the strike by ordering United
            States troops to Chicago because the strike
            was interfering with the United States mail
            and interstate commerce.

            July 20. The United States troops were re-
            moved from Chicago. The Pullman strike
            was called officially over by the American

Railway Union on August 3. It was a failure.

1895   November 2. The first contest between self-propelled vehicles in the United States was held at Chicago.

Eastern Illinois University was founded at Charleston and Northern Illinois University at De Kalb.

1896   July 11. The Democratic Party held its National Convention in Chicago. William Jennings Bryan was nominated for President and Arthur Sewall for Vice President.

Columbia College was founded at Chicago.

1897   January 11. John R. Tanner, Republican, who had been elected in 1896, became governor and served until the end of his term on January 14, 1901.

March 5. Lyman J. Gage became Secretary of the Treasury in the Cabinet of President William McKinley.

Bradley University was founded at Peoria.

1898   DePaul University was founded at Chicago, and Principia College at Elsah.

1899   Western Illinois University was founded at Macomb.

1900   Population: 4,821,550.

June 27-28. The Prohibitionist Party held its National Convention at Chicago. It nominated John G. Wooley for President and Henry B. Metcalf for Vice President.

1901   January 14. Richard Yates, Republican, who had been elected in 1900, became governor. He served in the office until January 9, 1905.

The state legislature passed an act establishing the initiative, providing that any question of public policy might be submitted to a popular vote if one-tenth of the registered voters of the state signed a petition requesting it.

1904   May 5. The Socialist Party's National Con-
              vention met in Chicago and nominated Eugene
              V. Debs for President and Benjamin Hanford
              for Vice President.

              June 21-23. The National Convention of the
              Republican Party met in Chicago where it
              nominated Theodore Roosevelt, the incumbent,
              for President and Charles W. Fairbanks for
              Vice President.

              July 1. Paul Morton became Secretary of the
              Navy in the Cabinet of President Theodore
              Roosevelt.

              July 4-5. The People's Party's National
              Convention met at Springfield and nominated
              Thomas E. Watson for President and Thomas H.
              Tibbles for Vice President.

              Child labor in the Illinois mines came to
              an end.

              The voters of the state approved the use of
              the secret "Australian" ballot for state
              primary elections.

1905   January 9. Charles S. Deneen, Republican,
              who had been elected in 1904, became gover-
              nor. He served in this office until February
              3, 1913, having been reelected in 1908.

1907   Olivet Nazarene College was established at
              Kankakee.

1908   The National Convention of the Socialist
              Party met at Chicago where it nominated
              Eugene V. Debs for President and Benjamin
              Hanford for Vice President. This was the
              same ticket as in 1904.

              June 16-20. The Republican Party's National
              Convention was held in Chicago. William H.
              Taft was nominated for President and James
              S. Sherman for Vice President.

              July 27. The Independence Party's National
              Convention met in Chicago, nominating Thomas
              L. Hisgen for President and John Temple
              Graves for Vice President.

              The state legislature passed a law providing
              for the direct nomination of all officers and

an "advisory" nomination of United States
Senators.

1909   March 5. Franklin MacVeagh was appointed
                Secretary of the Treasury in the Cabinet of
                President William Howard Taft. He assumed
                his office on March 8, 1909.

1910   Population: 5,638,591.

                January 24. Judge Landis began an investiga-
                tion of the beef trust in Chicago because
                of the raising of meat prices.

                March 1. The state legislature ratified the
                16th Amendment to the United States Consti-
                tution.

1911   March 7. Walter Lowrie Fisher became Secre-
                tary of the Interior in the Cabinet of
                President William Howard Taft.

                October 16. The National Conference of Pro-
                gressive Republicans met at Chicago and
                selected Robert M. La Follette as its presi-
                dential nominee.

                The state legislature passed the nation's
                first statewide law which provided for pay-
                ments from public funds for poor parents
                to aid them in the care of their children.

                Bethany Theological Seminary was founded at
                Oak Brook.

1912   June 18. The Republican National Convention
                met at Chicago. A violent split occurred
                between the followers of President Taft
                and those of former President Theodore
                Roosevelt. William Howard Taft was nominated
                for a second term. Theodore Roosevelt then
                announced the formation of the Progressive
                Party.

                Harriet Monroe began publication of her
                poetry in Chicago.

1913   February 3. Edward F. Dune, Democrat, who
                had been elected in 1912, became governor
                and served in the office until January 8,
                1917.

                February 13. The state legislature ratified

the 17th Amendment to the United States
Constitution.

July 5. At its convention in Chicago, the
National Association for the Advancement of
Colored People adopted a series of resolu-
tions which were designed to broaden its
direct action program.

August 12. The state legislature instituted
a State Highway Department.

The Northern Baptist Theological Seminary
was founded at Oak Brook.

1916   June 10. **The Progressive Party** met in National Convention at Chicago where it nominated Theodore Roosevelt for President and
John M. Parker for Vice President. Roosevelt
declined the nomination, indicating that he
preferred to support the Republican nominee,
Charles Evans Hughes.

1917   January 8. Frank O. Lowden, Republican, who
had been elected in 1916, became governor and
served until January 10, 1921. Governor
Lowden reorganized the Illinois government
through the passage of a consolidation act.

July 4. The first United States training
field for military aviators was opened at
Rantoul.

1919   January 14. The state legislature ratified
the Eighteenth Amendment to the United States
Constitution.

June 10. The state legislature ratified the
Nineteenth Amendment to the United States
Constitution. It was readopted on June 17.

August 31. The Communist Labor Party of
America was founded at Chicago. It adopted
the platform of the Third International.

Barat College was established at Lake Forest.

1920   Population: 6,485,280.

February 28. John Barton Payne was appointed
Secretary of the Interior in the Cabinet of
President Woodrow Wilson. He assumed his
office on March 13, 1920.

June 8-12. The Republican Party's National
Convention met at Chicago where it nominated
Warren G. Harding for President and Calvin
Coolidge for Vice President.

June 12. The Farmer Labor Party was founded
at a national convention in Chicago. It was
derived from a section of the National Labor
Party. The party joined forces with the
Progressive Party led by Robert La Follette
in 1924.

July 13-16. The National Convention of the
Farmer Labor Party met in Chicago where it
nominated Parley P. Christensen for President
and Max S. Hayes for Vice President.

1921 January 10. Leonard Small, Republican, who
had been elected in 1920, became governor.
He served in office until January 14, 1929,
having been reelected in 1924.

WDZ was the first radio station established
in the state at Tuscola. It later moved to
Decatur.

1922 A new state constitution was submitted to
the voters and was overwhelmingly rejected.

1924 March 18. One of the worst tornadoes in
the United States affected various towns
in Illinois.

July 10. The Worker's Party met in National
Convention at Chicago where it nominated
William Z. Foster for President and Benjamin
Gitlow for Vice President.

1925 George Frederick and Gladys Henry Dick of
Chicago developed an antitoxin for scarlet
fever.

1926 June 20. The first international Eucharistic
Congress in the United States met at Chicago.
Cardinal John Bonzano was named Papal
Legate a latere by Pope Pius XI.

1927 Spartus College of Judaica was established at
Chicago.

1928 July 11. The Farmer Labor Party's National
Convention met in Chicago where it nominated
George W. Norris for President and Will

Vereen for Vice President. When George
Norris declined Frank E. Webb became the
party's candidate.

July 12. The National Convention of the
Prohibition Party was held at Chicago. William F. Varney was nominated for President
and James A. Edgarton for Vice President.

1929   January 14. Louis L. Emmerson, Republican,
who had been elected in 1928, became governor and served in the office until January
9, 1933.

January 21. Roy O. West became Secretary of
the Interior in the Cabinet of President
Calvin Coolidge. He had been Secretary ad.
interim from July 23, 1928 to January 21,
1929.

March 5. James W. Good was appointed Secretary of War in the Cabinet of President Herbert Hoover. He assumed his office on March
6, 1929. Robert P. Lamont became Secretary
of Commerce in the Cabinet of President Hoover.

May 17. Al Capone was sentenced to one year
imprisonment at Chicago for carrying a con-
cealed weapon. He had pleaded guilty.

1930   Population: 7,630,654.

February 10. One of the largest rings of
bootleggers was exposed at Chicago since
the Prohibition Amendment went into effect.
It was estimated that this group had sold
over seven million gallons of whiskey to
speakeasies throughout the country. The
total business was thought to have totaled
approximately $50 million.

May 11. The Adler Planetarium opened in
Chicago. It was the first planetarium in
the nation.

Mundelein College was established at Chicago,
and the College of St. Francis at Joliet.

1932   April 21. The state legislature ratified
the Twentieth Amendment to the United States
Constitution.

May 28. The Communist Party held its National Convention at Chicago where it nominated William Z. Foster for President and James W. Ford, a black leader from New York City, for Vice President.

June 14-16. The Republican Party met in its National Convention at Chicago. It renominated President Herbert Hoover and Vice President Charles Curtis.

June 22. The state legislature ratified the Twentieth Amendment to the United States Constitution.

June 27-July 2. The Democratic National Convention met in Chicago Stadium. It nominated Governor Franklin D. Roosevelt of New York for President and John Nance Garner for Vice President. Roosevelt flew to Chicago to accept the nomination in a precedent-breaking move.

1933 January 9. Henry Horner, Democrat, who had been elected in 1932, became governor. He was reelected in 1936 and served until his death on October 6, 1940.

March 4. Harold L. Ickes became Secretary of the Interior in the Cabinet of President Franklin D. Roosevelt.

June 22. The Illinois Ship Canal was formally opened linking the Great Lakes with the Guld of Mexico.

July 10. The state legislature ratified the Twenty-first Amendment to the United States Constitution.

The "Century of Progress" Exposition was held at Chicago. It provided the first large-scale presentation of modern architectural aims and methods in the nation.

1940 Population: 7,897,241.

May 10 The Prohibition Party held its National Convention in Chicago, nominating Roger W. Babson for President and Edgar V. Moorman for Vice President.

July 10. Frank Knox became Secretary of the

Navy in the Cabinet of President Franklin D.
Roosevelt.

July 15-19. The National Convention of the
Democratic Party met at Chicago. It renominated President Franklin D. Roosevelt
for a third term as President and nominated
Henry A. Wallace for Vice President.

October 6. Lieutenant Governor John Stelle,
Democrat, became governor upon the death
of Governor Henry Horner.

WBBM-TV began broadcasting as the first
television station in the state at Chicago.

1941   January 13. Dwight H. Green, Republican,
who had been elected in 1940, became governor. He served in the office until January
10, 1949, having been reelected in 1944.

1942   December 2. The Atomic Age began when Enrico
Fermi and other scientists at the University
of Chicago were able to achieve the first
controlled atomic chain reaction.

1943   October 16. Chicago dedicated its first
passenger subway.

1944   June 26-28. The Republican Party held its
National Convention at Chicago where it
nominated Thomas E. Dewey for President and
John Bricker for Vice President.

July 19-21. The National Convention of the
Democratic Party met in Chicago where it
renominated President Franklin D. Roosevelt
for a fourth term and nominated Harry S.
Truman for Vice President.

1945   Roosevelt College was founded as Thomas
Jefferson College in Chicago. The first
classes were held the same year. The name
of Roosevelt College was adopted in 1954.

1946   Parks College of Aeronautical Technology of
St. Louis University was founded at Cahokia.

1947   April 3. The state legislature ratified the
Twenty-second Amendment to the United States
Constitution.

Illinois College of Optometry was founded

at Chicago.

1949   January 10. Adlai E. Stevenson, Democrat,
who had been elected in 1948, became governor. He served in the office until January
12, 1953.

1950   Population: 8,712,176.

Lewis University was founded at Lockport.

1952   July 11. The Progressive Party's National
Convention met in Chicago where Vincent
Hallinon was nominated for President and
Charlotte A. Bass for Vice President.

July 26. At the Democratic National Convention in Chicago Adlai E. Stevenson was nominated for President and Senator John J.
Sparkman for Vice President.

Trinity College was established at Deerfield.

1953   January 12. William G. Stratton, Republican,
who had been elected in 1952, became governor.
He was reelected in 1956 and served until
January 9, 1961.

1954   October 9-10. Torrential rains filled the
rivers and flooded part of the Chicago Loop
business area.

1956   June 8-10. At the 30th National Convention
of the Socialist Party in Chicago Darlington
Hoopes was nominated for President.

June 11. The American Medical Association,
meeting in Chicago, heard reports from Dr.
Jonas Salk and Surgeon General Leonard A.
Scheele that paralytic polio would be elim-
inated as a threat within three years with
the help of the Salk vaccine.

August 13-17. The Democratic National Con-
vention met at Chicago where it nominated
Adlai E. Stevenson for President and Senator
Estes Kefauver for Vice President.

1960   Population: 10,081,158.

One of the largest nuclear reactors in the
United States was completed at Dresden.

1961   January 9. Otto Kerner, Jr, Democrat, who
            had been elected in 1960, became governor.
            He was reelected in 1964 and served until
            his resignation on May 22, 1968.

            January 21. Arthur J. Goldberg became Sec-
            retary of Labor in the Cabinet of President
            John F. Kennedy.

            March 14. The state legislature ratified
            the Twenty-third Amendment to the United
            States Constitution.

            September 1. A Trans World Airlines con-
            stellation crashed in Hillsdale four minutes
            after take-off from Chicago's Midway Air-
            port. 78 persons were killed in what was
            described as United States commercial avia-
            tion's worst single plane crash.

            The state legislature established the Board
            of Higher Education to coordinate the work of
            Illinois' numerous public colleges and uni-
            versities.

            The United States Supreme Court ruled a Chicago
            ordinance forbidding the showing of any mo-
            tion picture without permission of the city
            censors constitutional.

1962   September 20. W. Willard Wirtz was appointed
            Secretary of Labor in the Cabinet of Presi-
            dent John F. Kennedy. He assumed his office
            on September 25, 1962.

            November 14. Illinois became the first state
            to ratify the Twenty-fourth Amendment to the
            United States Constitution.

            December 23. The Illinois Public Aid Com-
            mission approved a policy whereby married
            women or unmarried mothers on state relief
            rolls could request and receive contracep-
            tive devices and birth control information.

            Mrs. Edith Sampson became the first Black
            woman elected to a judgeship in the state.
            She was to become a municipal judge in
            Chicago.

1963   October 22. A one-day school boycott occurred
            to protest defacto school segregation. About
            225,000 students were absent from the Chicago

public schools.

The state government established a birth control program.

Judson College was founded at Elgin.

1964   July 26. James R. Hoffa, president of the International Brotherhood of Teamsters and six other officers were convicted of fraud and conspiracy in their management of the union pension fund by a federal jury in Chicago.

The citizens of the state approved a constitutional amendment which streamlined the working and administration of the Illinois court system.

1965   February 10. Nicholas De B. Katzenbach was confirmed as Attorney General in the Cabinet of President Lyndon B. Johnson. Katzenbach had been ad interim Attorney General since September 4, 1964. He officially assumed his duties on February 11.

July 24-26. Dr. Martin Luther King, Jr. led a civil rights campaign in the various Black neighborhoods of Chicago as well as in the white suburb of Winnetka. He and his followers claimed that Winnetka was a "symbol of defacto segregation."

A panel of federal and state judges carried out a reapportionment of the state Senate. In addition a special commission reapportioned the state House of Representatives.

The state legislature passed a junior college act which prepared the way for establishment of a network of community colleges.

1966   The Atomic Energy Commission chose the small town of Weston as the site for its 200 billion electron volt accelerator.

1967   March 22. The state legislature ratified the Twenty-fifth Amendment to the United States Constitution.

1968   May 22. Lieutenant Governor Samuel H. Shaping, Democrat, became governor and served until the end of the term on January 13, 1969.

Governor Otto Kerner had resigned on this
date.

May 26-29.   The Democratic Party held its
National Convention at Chicago, where it
nominated Hubert H. Humphrey, present Vice
President of the United States, for Presi-
dent and Edmund S. Muskie for Vice President.
A great deal of rioting occurred over the
United States' involvement in Vietnam.

1969   January 13.   Richard B. Ogilvie, Republican,
who had been elected in 1968, became gover-
nor.   He served in the office until the end
of his term on January 8, 1973.

January 20.   George P. Shultz was appointed
Secretary of Labor in the Cabinet of President Richard M. Nixon.   Schultz entered upon
his duties on January 22.   On this same date
David M. Kennedy was appointed Secretary of
the Treasury in President Nixon's Cabinet.
He also assumed his office on January 22.

The Illinois legislature adopted individual
and corporate income taxes.

The Catholic Theological Union was founded
at Chicago.

1970   Population: 11,113,976.

Illinois voters approved a bond issue for
$750,000,000 for improvement of sewage dis-
posal and for fighting water pollution.

1971   June 24.   The state legislature ratified the
Twenty-sixth Amendment to the United States
Constitution.

July 1.   A new state constitution which the
voters had approved in 1970 went into effect.

1972   January 27.   Peter G. Peterson was appointed
Secretary of Commerce in the Cabinet of
President Richard M. Nixon.   He entered upon
his duties on February 21, 1972.

March 24.   The Illinois Supreme Court upheld
the ruling of a lower court that no-fault
insurance was unconstitutional because it
discriminated against the poor.

May 16. George P. Shultz was appointed Secretary of the Treasury in the Cabinet of
President Richard M. Nixon. He assumed his
office on June 12, 1972.

Garret-Evangelical Theological Seminary was
founded at Evanston, and VanderCook College
of Music at Chicago.

1973   January 8. Daniel Walker, Democrat, who had
              been elected in 1972, became governor.

              September 5. Governor Walker vetoed a no-
              fault insurance bill which had been passed
              by the state legislature.

              The world's tallest building, the 1,454-foot
              Sears Tower, was completed in Chicago.

1975   The state legislature defeated the proposed
              Equal Rights Amendment.

1976   September 14. The United States Civil Rights
              Commission indicated that the integration
              of the Joliet school system was proceeding
              satisfactorily.

              November 2. James R. Thompson, Republican,
              was elected governor of the state. He began
              serving in the office in 1977.

1977   February 15. The Justice Department filed
              a civil antitrust suit aginst the Illinois
              Podiatry Society. It charged thet the
              "relative-value" guides which had been a-
              dopted to determine fees had provided a
              means by which the group was able to re-
              strict fee competition and thus violated
              the federal antitrust laws.

              May 16. The United States Supreme Court
              upheld an Illinois traffic law which per-
              mitted state authorities to automatically
              revoke a driver's license, without prior
              hearing, if it had been suspended three
              times within a ten-year period.

              June 6. The Illinois House defeated the
              federal Equal Rights Amendment.

BIOGRAPHICAL DIRECTORY

The selected list og governors, United States Senators and members of the House of Representatives for
Illinois, 1800-1977, includes all persons listed in the
Chronology for whom basic biographical data was readily
available. Older biographical sources are frequently
in conflict on certain individuals, and in such cases
the source most commonly cited by later authorities was
preferred.

ADAIR, Jackson Leroy
    Republican
    b. Clayton, Ill., February 23, 1887
    d. Quincy, Ill., January 19, 1956
    U. S. Representative, 1933-37

ADAMS, George Everett
    Republican
    b. Keene, N. H., June 18, 1840
    d. Petersborough, N. H., October 5, 1917
    U. S. Representative, 1883-91

ADKINS, Charles
    Republican
    b. Pickaway County, Ohio, February 7, 1863
    d. Decatur, Illinois, March 31, 1941
    U. S. Representative, 1925-33

ALDRICH, James Franklin
    Republican
    b. Two Rivers, Wis., April 6, 1853
    d. Chicago, Ill., March 8, 1933
    U. S. Representative, 1893-97

ALDRICH, William
    Republican
    b. Greenfield Center, N. Y., January 19, 1820
    d. Fond du Lac, Wis., December 3, 1885
    U. S. Representative, 1877-83

ALLEN, James Cameron
    Democrat
    b. Shelby County, Ky., January 29, 1822
    d. Olney, Ill., January 30, 1912
    U. S. Representative, 1853-56, 1856-57, 1863-65

ALLEN, John Clayton
    Republican
    b. Hinesbury, Vt., February 14, 1860
    d. Monmouth, Ill., January 12, 1939
    U. S. Representative, 1925-33

ALLEN, Leo Elwood
    Republican
    b. Elizabeth, Ill., October 5, 1898
    U. S. Representative, 1933-61

ALLEN, William Joshua
    Democrat

b. Wilson County, Tenn., June 9, 1829
d. Hot Springs, Ark., January 26, 1901
U. S. Representative, 1862-65

ALLEN, Willis
    Democrat
    b. Roanoke, Va., December 15, 1806
    d. Harrisburg, Ill., April 15, 1859
    U. S. Representative, 1851-55

Altgeld, John P.
    Democrat
    b. Germany, 1847
    d. 1902
    Governor of Illinois, 1893-97

ANDERSON, George Alburtas
    Democrat
    b. Botetourt County, Va., March 11, 1853
    d. Quincy, Ill., January 31, 1896
    U. S. Representative, 1887-89

ANDERSON, John Bayard
    Republican
    b. Rockford, Ill., February 15, 1922
    U. S. Representative, 1961-

ANDERSON, William Black
    Democrat
    b. Mt. Vernon, Ill., April 2, 1830
    d. Chicago, Ill., August 28, 1901
    U. S. Representative, 1875-77

ANNUNZIO, Frank
    Democrat
    b. Chicago, Ill., January 12, 1915
    U. S. Representative, 1965-

ARENDS, Leslie Cornelias
    Republican
    b. Melvin, Ill., September 27, 1895
    U. S. Representative, 1935-

ARNOLD, Isaac Newton
    b. Hartwick, N. Y., November 30, 1815
    d. Chicago, Ill., April 24, 1884
    U. S. Representative, 1861-65

ARNOLD, Laurence Fletcher
    Democrat
    b. Newton, Ill., June 8, 1891
    d. Newton, Ill., December 6, 1966
    U. S. Representative, 1937-43

ARNOLD, William Wright
    Democrat
    b. Oblong, Ill., October 14, 1877
    d. Robinson, Ill., November 23, 1957
    U. S. Representative, 1923-35

BAGBY, John Courts
    Democrat
    b. Glasgow, Ky., January 24, 1819
    d. Rushville, Ill., April 4, 1896
    U. S. Representative, 1875-77

BAKER, David Jewett
    Democrat
    b. East Haddam, Conn., September 7, 1792
    d. Alton, Ill., August 6, 1869
    U. S. Senator, 1830

BAKER, Edward Dickinson
    Republican
    b. London, England, February 24, 1811
    d. Battle of Balls Bluff, Va., October 21, 1861
    U. S. Representative, 1845-47 (Whig),
        1849-51 (Republican)

BAKER, Jehu
    Republican
    b. near Lexington, Ky., November 22, 1822
    d. Belleville, Ill., March 1, 1903
    U. S. Representative, 1865-69, 1887-89 (Republican)
        1897-99 (Fusionist)

BALTZ William Nicholas
    Democrat
    b. Millstadt, Ill., February 5, 1860
    d. Millstadt, Ill., August 22, 1943
    U. S. Representative, 1913-15

BARBER, Hiram, Jr.
    Republican
    b. Queensbury, N. Y., March 24, 1835
    d. Lake Geneva, Wis., August 5, 1924
    U. S. Representative, 1879-81

BARNES, James Martin
    Democrat
    b. Jacksonville, Ill., January 9, 1899
    d. Washington, D. C., June 8, 1958
    U. S. Representative, 1939-43

BARRERE, Granville
    b. New Market, Ohio, July 11, 1829
    d. Canton, Ill., January 13, 1889

BARRERE, Nelson
    Whig
    b. New Market, Ohio, April 1, 1808
    d. Hillsboro, Ohio, August 20, 1883
    U. S. Representative, 1851-53

BEAM, Harry Peter
    Democrat
    b. Peoria, Ill., November 23, 1892
    U. S. Representative, 1931-32

BELKNAP, Hugh Reid
    Representative
    b. Keokuk, Iowa, September 1, 1860
    d. Calamba, Philippine Islands, November 12, 1901
    U. S. Representative, 1895-99

BEVERIDGE, John Lourie
    Republican
    b. Greenwich, N. Y., July 6, 1824
    d. Hollywood, Calif., May 3, 1910
    U. S. Representative, 1871-73
    Governor of Illinois, 1873-77

BISHOP, Cecil William
    Republican
    b. near West Vienna, Ill., June 29, 1890
    U. S. Representative, 1941-55

BISSELL, William Harrison
    Republican
    b. Hartwick, N. Y., April 25, 1811
    d. Springfield, Ill., March 18, 1860
    U. S. Representative, 1849-55
    Governor of Illinois, 1857-60

BLACK, John Charles
    Democrat
    b. Lexington, Ill., January 27, 1839
    d. Chicago, Ill., August 17,1915
    U. S. Representative, 1893-95

BOND, Shardach
    Democrat
    b. Frederick, Md., November 24, 1773
    d. Kaskaskia, Ill., April 12, 1832
    U. S. Representative (Territorial Delegate), 1812-14
    Governor of Illinois, 1818-22

BORCHERS, Charles Martin
    Democrat
    b. Lockville, Ohio, November 18, 1869
    d. Decatur, Ill., December 2, 1946

U. S. Representative, 1913-15

BOUTELL, Henry Sherman
    Republican
    b. Boston, Mass., March 14, 1856
    d. San Remo, Italy, March 11, 1926
    U. S. Representative, 1897-1911

BOWLER, James Bernard
    Democrat
    b. Chicago, Ill., February 5, 1875
    d. Chicago, Ill., July 18, 1957
    U. S. Representative, 1953-57

BOYD, Thomas Alexander
    Republican
    b. near Bedford, Pa.
    d. Lewiston, Ill., May 28, 1897
    U. S. Representative, 1877-81

BOYER, Lewis Leonard
    Democrat
    b. near Richfield, Richfield Township, Ill., May 19,
        1886
    d. Quincy, Ill., March 12, 1944
    U. S. Representative, 1937-39

BOYLE, Charles Augustus
    Democrat
    b. Spring Lake, Mich., August 13, 1907
    d. Chicago, Ill., November 4, 1959
    U. S. Representative, 1955-59

BREESE, Didney
    Democrat
    b. Whitesboro, N. Y., July 15, 1800
    d. Pinkneyville, Ill., June 28, 1878
    U. S. Senator, 1843-49

BRENNAN, Martin Adlai
    Democrat
    b. Bloomington, Ill., September 21, 1879
    d. Frederick, Md., July 4, 1941
    U. S. Representative, 1933-39

BRENTANO, Lorenzo
    Republican
    b. Manneheim, Grand Duchy of Baden, Germany, Novem-
        ber 4, 1813
    d. Chicago, Ill., September 18, 1891
    U. S. Representative, 1877-79

BRITTEN, Frederick Albert
    Republican
    b. Chicago, Ill., November 18, 1871
    d. Bethesda, Md., May 4, 1946
    U. S. Representative, 1915-35

BROMWELL, Henry Pelham Holmes
    Republican
    b. Baltimore, Md., August 26, 1823
    d. Denver, Colo., January 7, 1903
    U. S. Representative, 1865-69

BROOKS, Charles Wayland
    Republican
    b. West Bureau, Ill., March 8, 1897
    d. Chicago, Ill., January 14, 1957
    U. S. Senator, 1940-49

BROOKS, Edwin Bruce
    Republican
    b. Newton, Ill., September 20, 1868
    d. Newton, Ill., September 18, 1933
    U. S. Representative, 1919-23

BROWNING, Orville Hickman
    Republican
    b. Cynthiana, Tenn., February 10, 1806
    d. Quincy, Ill., August 10, 1881
    U. S. Senator, 1861-63
    Secretary of the Interior, 1866-69
    U. S. Attorney General, 1868

BUCHANAN, Frank
    Democrat
    b. near Madison, Ind., June 14, 1862
    d. Chicago, Ill., April 18, 1830
    U. S. Representative, 1911-17

BUCKBEE, John Theodore
    Republican
    b. near Rockford, Ill., August 1, 1871
    d. Rockford, Ill., April 23, 1936
    U. S. Representative, 1927-36

BUCKLEY, James Richard
    Democrat
    b. Chicago, Ill., November 18, 1870
    d. Chicago, Ill., June 22, 1945
    U. S. Representative, 1923-25

BUCKLEY, James Vincent
    Democrat
    b. Saginaw County, Michigan, May 15, 1894

      d. Hammond, Ind., July 30, 1954
      U. S. Representative, 1949-51

BURCHARD, Harold Chapin
      Republican
      b. Marshall, N. Y., September 22, 1825
      d. Freeport, Ill., May 14, 1908
      U. S. Representative, 1869-79

BURR, Albert George
      Democrat
      b. near Batavia, N. Y., November 8, 1829
      d. Carrollton, Ill., June 10, 1882
      U. S. Representative, 1867-71

BURRELL, Orlando
      Republican
      b. Newton, Pa., July 26, 1826
      d. Carmi, Ill., June 7, 1922
      U. S. Representative, 1895-97

BUSBEY, Fred Ernst
      Republican
      b. Tuscola, Ill., February 8, 1895
      d. Cocoa Beach, Fla., February 11, 1966
      U. S. Representative, 1943-45, 1947-49, 1951-55

BUSEY, Samuel Thompson
      Democrat
      b. Greencastle, Ind.
      d. Urbana, Ill.
      U. S. Representative, 1891-93

BYRNE, Emmet Francis
      Republican
      b. Chicago, Ill., December 6, 1896
      U. S. Representative, 1957-59

CABLE, Benjamin Taylor
      Democrat
      b. Georgetown, Ky., August 11, 1853
      d. Rock Island, Ill., December 13, 1923
      U. S. Representative, 1891-93

CALDWELL, Ben Franklin
      Democrat
      b. near Carrollton, Ill., August 2, 1848
      d. Springfield, Ill., December 29, 1924
      U. S. Representative, 1899-1905, 1907-07

CAMPBELL, Alexander
      Independent
      b. near Concord, Pa., October 4, 1814

d. La Salle, Ill., August 8, 1898
U. S. Representative, 1875-77

CAMPBELL, James Romulus
Democrat
b. near McLeansboro, Ill., May 4, 1853
d. McLeansboro, Ill., August 12, 1924
U. S. Representative, 1897-99

CANNON, Joseph Gurney
Republican
b. Guilford, N. C., May 7, 1836
d. Danville, Ill., November 12, 1926
U. S. Representative, 1873-91, 1893-1913, 1915-23
    Speaker, 1903-11

CARLIN, Thomas
Democrat
b. Fayette County, Ky., July 18, 1789
d. February 14, 1852
Governor of Illinois, 1838-1842

CASEY, Zadoc
Jackson Democrat
b. Greene County, Ga., March 7, 1740
d. Caseyville, Ill., September 4, 1862
U. S. Representative, 1833-43

CAULFIELD, Bernatd Gregory
Democrat
b. Alexandria, Va., October 18, 1828
d. Deadwood (Territory of Dakota), now S. D.,
    May 11, 1877
U. S. Representative, 1875-77

CHAMPION, Edwin Van Meter
Democrat
b. Mansfield, Ill., September 13, 1890
U. S. Representative, 1937-39

CHAPMAN, Pleasant Thomas
Republican
b. near Vienna, Ill, October 8, 1854
d. Vienna, Ill., January 31, 1931
U. S. Representative, 1905-11

CHESNEY, Chester Anton
Democrat
b. Chicago, Ill., March 9, 1916
U. S. Representative, 1949-51

CHILDES, Robert Andrew
Republican

b. Malone, N. Y., March 22, 1845
d. Hinsdale, Ill., December 19, 1815
U. S. Representative, 1893-95

CHINDBLOM, Carl Richard
Republican
b. Chicago, Ill., December 21, 1870
d. Chicago, Ill., September 12, 1956
U. S. Representative, 1919-33

CHIPERFIELD, Burnett Mitchell
Republican
b. Dover, Ill., June 14, 1870
d. Canton, Ill., June 24, 1940
U. S. Representative, 1915-16, 1929-33

CHIPERFIELD, Robert Bruce
Republican
b. Canton, Ill., November 20, 1899
d. Canton, Ill., April 9, 1971
U. S. Representative, 1939-63

CHURCH, Marguerite Shitt
Republican
b. New York, N. Y., September 13, 1892
U. S. Representative, 1951-63

CHURCH, Ralph Edwin
Republican
b. near Catlin, Ill., May 5, 1883
d. Washington, D. C., March 21, 1950
U. S. Representative, 1935-41, 1943-50

CLEMENTS, Isaac
Republican
b. near Brookville, Ind., March 31, 1837
d. Danville, Ill., May 31, 1909
U. S. Representative, 1873-75

CLIPPINGER, Ray
Republican
b. Fairfield, Ill., January 13, 1886
d. Carmi, Ill., December 24, 1962
U. S. Representative, 1945-49

COLES, Edward
Democrat-Republican
b. Albemarle County, Va., December 15, 1786
d. July 7, 1868
Governor of Illinois, 1822-26

COLLIER, Harold Reginald
Republican

b. Lansing, Mich., December 12, 1915
U. S. Representative, 1957-

COLLINS, George Washington
Democrat
b. Chicago, Ill., March 5, 1925
U. S. Representative, November 3, 1970-

CONNOLLY, James Austin
Republican
b. Newark, N. J., March 8, 1843
d. Springfield, Ill., December 15, 1914
U. S. Representative, 1895-99

COOK, Burton Chauncey
Republican
b. Pittsford, N. Y., May 11, 1819
d. Evanston, Ill., August 18, 1894
U. S. Representative, 1865-71

COOK, Daniel Pope
b. Scott County, Ky., 1794
d. Scott County, Ky., October 16, 1827
U. S. Representative, 1819-27

COOKE, Edward Dean
Republican
b. Cascade, Iowa, October 17, 1849
d. Washington, D. C., June 24, 1897
U. S. Representative, 1895-97

COPLEY, Ira Clifton
Republican
b. Galesburg, Ill., October 25, 1864
d. Aurora, Ill., November 1, 1947
U. S. Representative, 1911-23

CORWIN, Franklin
Republican
b. Lebanon, Ohio, January 12, 1818
d. Peru, Ill., June 15, 1879
U. S. Representative, 1873-75

CREBS, John Montgomery
b. Middlebury, Va., April 9, 1830
d. Carmi, Ill., June 26, 1890
U. S. Representative, 1869-73

CULLEN, William
    Republican
    b. County Donegal, Ireland, March 4, 1820
    d. Ottawa, Ill., January 17, 1914
    U. S. Representative, 1881-85

CULLOM, Shelby Moore
    Republican
    b. Wayne County, Ky., November 22, 1824
    d. Washington, D. C., January 28, 1914
    U. S. Representative, 1865-71
    Governor of Illinois, 1877-83
    U. S. Senator, 1883-1913

CUNNINGHAM, Paul Harvey
    Republican
    b. Indiana County, near Kent, Pa., June 15, 1890
    d. Gull Lake, Brainerd, Minn., July 18, 1961
    U. S. Representative, 1941-59

CUSACK, Thomas
    Democrat
    b. Kilrush, County Clare, Ireland, October 5, 1858
    d. Chicago, Ill., November 19, 1926
    U. S. Representative, 1899-1901

DAVIS, David
    Independent/Democrat
    b. near Cecilton, Md., March 9, 1815
    d. Bloomington, Ill., June 26, 1886
    U. S. Senator, 1877-83, President pro tempore,
        1881-83
    Associate Justice of the U. S. Supreme Court, 1862-
        77

DAVIS, George Royal
    Republican
    b. Palmer, Mass., January 3, 1840
    d. Chicago, Ill., November 25, 1899
    U. S. Representative, 1879-85

DAVIS, Jacob Cunningham
    Democrat
    b. near Staunton, Va., September 16, 1820
    d. Alexanderia, Me., December 25, 1883
    U. S. Representative, 1856-57

DAWSON, William Levi
    Democrat
    b. Albany, Ga., April 26, 1886
    d. Chicago, Ill., November 9, 1970
    U. S. Representative, 1943-1970

DAY, Stephen Albion
    Republican
    b. Canton, Ohio, July 13, 1882
    d. Evanston, Ill., January 5, 1950
    U. S. Representative, 1941-45

DENEEN, Charles Samuel
    Republican
    b. Edwardsville, Ill., May 4, 1863
    d. Chicago, Ill., February 5, 1940
    Governor of Illinois, 1905-13
    U. S. Senator, 1925-31

DENISON, Edward Everett
    Republican
    b. Marion, Ill., August 28, 1873
    d. Carbondale, Ill., June 17, 1953
    U. S. Representative, 1915-31

DE PRIEST, Oscar
    Republican
    b. Florence, Ala., March 9, 1871
    d. Chicago, Ill., May 12, 1951
    U. S. Representative, 1929-35

DERWINSKI, Edward Joseph
    Republican
    b. Chicago, Ill., September 15, 1926
    U. S. Representative, 1959-

DEWEY, Charles Schuveldt
    Republican
    b. Cadiz, Ohio, November 10, 1882
    U. S. Representative, 1941-45

DICKSON, Frank Stoddard
    Republican
    b. Hillsboro, Ill., October 6, 1876
    d. Washington, D. C., February 24, 1953
    U. S. Representative, 1905-07

DIETERICH, William Henry
    Democrat
    b. near Cooperstown, N.Y., March 31, 1876
    d. Springfield, Ill., October 12, 1940
    U. S. Representative, 1931-33
    U. S. Senator, 1933-39

DIRKSEN, Everett McKinley
    Republican
    b. Pekin, Ill., January 4, 1896
    d. Washington, D. C., September 7, 1969
    U. S. Representative, 1933-49

U. S. Senator, 1951-69

DOBBINS, Donald Claude
    Democrat
    b. near Dewey, Ill., March 20, 1878
    d. Champaign, Ill., February 14, 1943
    U. S. Representatuve, 1933-39.

DOUGLAS, Emily Taft
    Democrat
    b. Chicago, April 10, 1899
    U. S. Representative, 1945-47

DOUGLAS, Paul Howard
    Democrat
    b. near Salem, Mass., March 26, 1892
    U. S. Senator, 1949-67

DOUGLAS, Stephen Arnold
    Popular Sovereignty Democrat
    b. Brandon, Vt., April 23, 1813
    d. Chicago, Ill., June 3, 1861
    U. S. Representative, 1843-47 (Democrat)
    U. S. Senator, 1847-53 (Democrat), 1853-61 (popu-
        lar Sovereignty Democrat)

DOWNING, Finis Ewing
    Democrat
    b. Virginia, Ill., August 24, 1846
    d. Virginia, Ill., March 8, 1936
    U. S. Representative, 1895-96

DOYLE, Thomas Aloysius
    Democrat
    b. Chicago, Ill., January 6, 1886
    d. Chicago, Ill., January 29, 1935
    U. S. Representative, 1923-31

DUNCAN, Joseph
    Jackson Democrat
    b. Paris, Ky., February 22, 1794
    d. Jacksonville, Ill., January 15, 1844
    U. S. Representative, 1827-34
    Governor of Illinois, 1834-38

DUNHAM, Ransom Williams
    Republican
    b. Savoy, Mass., March 21, 1838
    d. Savoy, Mass., August 19, 1896
    U. S. Representative, 1883-89

DUNNE, Edward F.
    Democrat

b. Waterville, Conn., October 12, 1853
d. May 24, 1937
Governor of Illinois, 1913-17

BURBOROW, Alan Cathcard, Jr.
    Democrat
    b. Philadelphia, Pa., November 10, 1857
    d. Chicago, Ill., March 10, 1908
    U. S. Representative, 1891-95

EDEN, John Rice
    Democrat
    b. Bath County, Ky., February 1, 1826
    d. Sullivan, Ill., June 9, 1909
    U. S. Representative, 1863-65, 1873-79, 1885-87

EDWARDS, Ninian
    Democrat
    b. "Mount Pleasant," Montgomery County, Md., March
        17, 1775
    d. Springfield, Ill., July 20, 1833
    Territorial Governor of Illinois, 1809-18
    U. S. Senator, 1818-24
    Governor of Illinois, 1826-31

ELLWOOD, Reuben
    Republican
    b. Minden, N. Y., February 21, 1821
    d. Sycamore, Ill., July 1, 1885
    U. S. Representative, 1883-85

EMERICH, Martin
    Democrat
    b. Baltimore, Md., April 27, 1846
    d. New York, N. Y., September 27, 1922
    U. S. Representative, 1903-05

EMMERSON, Louis L.
    Republican
    b. Albion, Ill., December 27, 1863
    d. February 4, 1941
    Governor of Illinois, 1929-33

ERLENBORN, John N.
    Republican
    b. Chicago, Ill., February 8, 1927
    U. S. Representative, 1965-

EVANS, Lynden
    Democrat
    b. La Salle, Ill., June 28, 1858
    d. Chicago, Ill., May 6, 1926
    U. S. Representative, 1911-13

EWING, William Lee Davidson
 Jackson Democrat
 b. Paris, Ky., August 31, 1795
 d. Vandalia, Ill., March 25, 1846
 Governor of Illinois, 1834
 U. S. Senator, 1835-37

FARNSWORTH, John Franklin
 Republican
 b. Eaton, Canada, March 27, 1820
 d. Washington, D. C., July 14, 1897
 U. S. Representative, 1857-61, 1863-73

FARWELL, Charles Benjamin
 Republican
 b. Painted Post, N. Y., July 1, 1823
 d. Lake Forest, Ill., September 23, 1903
 U. S. Representative, 1871-76, 1881-83
 U. S. Senator, 1887-91

FEELY, John Joseph
 Democrat
 b. near Wilmington, Ill., August 1, 1875
 d. Chicago, Ill., February 15, 1905
 U. S. Representative, 1901-03

FICKLIN, Orlando Bell
 Democrat
 b. Scott County, Ky., December 16, 1808
 d. Charleston, Ill., May 5, 1886
 U. S. Representative, 1843-49, 1851-53

FIFER, Joseph W.
 Republican
 b. Staunton, Va., October 28, 1840
 d. August 6, 1938
 Governor of Illinois, 1889-93

FINDLEY, Paul
 Republican
 b. Jacksonville, Ill., June 23, 1921
 U. S. Representative, 1961-

FINERTY, John Frederick
 Independent Democrat
 b. Galway, Ireland, September 10, 1846
 d. Chicago, Ill., June 10, 1908
 U. S. Representative, 1883-85

FINNEGAN, Edward Rowan
 Democrat
 b. Chicago, Ill., June 5, 1905
 d. Chicago, Ill., February 2, 1971
 U. S. Representative, 1961-64

FITHIAN, George Washington
    Democrat
    b. Willow Hill, Ill., July 4, 1854
    d. Memphis, Tenn., January 21, 1921
    U. S. Representative, 1889-95

FITZHENRY, Louis
    Democrat
    b. Bloomington, Ill., June 13, 1870
    d. Normal, Ill., November 18, 1935
    U. S. Representative, 1913-15

FORD, Thomas
    Democrat
    b. Fayette County, Pa., December 5, 1800
    d. November 3, 1850
    Governor of Illinois, 1842-46

FORMAN, William S. John
    Democrat
    b. Natchez, Miss., January 20, 1847
    d. Champaign, Ill., June 10, 1908
    U. S. Representative, 1889-95

FORSYTHE, Albert Palaska
    Republican
    b. New Richmond, Ohio, May 24, 1830
    d. Independence, Kans., September 2, 1906
    U. S. Representative, 1879-81

FORT, Greenbury Lafayette
    Republican
    b. French Grant, Ohio, October 17, 1825
    d. Lacon, Ill., January 13, 1883

FOSS, George Edmund
    Republican
    b. West Berkshire, Vt., July 2, 1863
    d. Chicago, Ill., March 15, 1936
    U. S. Representative, 1895-1913, 1915-19

FOSTER, George Peter
    b. Dover, N. J., April 3, 1858
    d. Wharton, Ill., November 11, 1928
    U. S. Representative, 1899-1905

FOSTER, Martin David
    Democrat
    b. West Salem, Ill., September 3, 1861
    d. Olney, Ill., October 20, 1919
    U. S. Representative, 1907-19

FOUKE, Philip Bond
     Democrat
     b. Kaskaskia, Ill., January 23, 1818
     d. Washington, D. C., October 3, 1876
     U. S. Representative, 1859-63

FOWLER, Hiram Robert
     Democrat
     b. Eddyville, Ill., February 7, 1851
     d. Harrisburg, Ill., January 5, 1926
     U. S. Representative, 1911-15

FRENCH, Augustus C.
     Democrat
     b. New Hampshire, August 2, 1808
     d. September 4, 1864
     Governor of Illinois, 1846-53

FRIES, Frank William
     Democrat
     b. Hornsby, Ill., May 1, 1893
     U. S. Representative, 1937-41

FULLER, Charles Eugene
     Republican
     b. near Belvidere, Ill., March 31, 1849
     d. Rochester, Minn., June 25, 1926
     U. S. Representative, 1903-13, 1915-26

FUNK, Benjamin Franklin
     Republican
     b. Funks Grove Township, Ill., October 17, 1838
     d. Bloomington, Ill., February 14, 1909
     U. S. Representative, 1893-95

FUNK, Frank Hamilton
     Republican
     b. Bloomington, Ill, April 5, 1869
     d. Bloomington, Ill., November 24, 1940
     U. S. Representative, 1921-27

GALLAGHER, Thomas
     Democrat
     b. Concord, N. H., July 6, 1850
     d. San Antonio, Tex., February 24, 1930
     U. S. Representative, 1909-21

GEST, William Harrison
     Republican
     b. Jacksonville, Ill, January 7, 1838
     d. Rock Island, Ill., August 9, 1912
     U. S. Representative, 1887-91

GILLESPIE, James Frank
    Democrat
    b. White Sulphur Springs, W. Va., April 18, 1869
    d. Bloomington, Ill., Novemner 26, 1954
    U. S. Representative, 1933-35

GLENN, Otis Ferguson
    Republican
    b. Mattoon, Ill., August 27, 1879
    d. Portage Point, near Onekama, Mich., March 11,
        1959
    U. S. Senator, 1928-33

GOLDZIER, Julius
    Democrat
    b. Vienna Austria, January 20, 1854
    d. Chicago, Ill., January 20, 1925
    U. S. Representative, 1893-95

GORDON, Thomas Sylvy
    Democrat
    b. Chicago, Ill., December 17, 1893
    d. Chicago Ill., January 22, 1959
    U. S. Representative, 1943-49

GORMAN, George Edmund
    Democrat
    b. Chicago, Ill., April 13, 1873
    d. Chicago, Ill., January 13, 1935
    U. S. Representative, 1913-15

GORMAN, John Jerome
    Republican
    b. Minneapolis, Minn., June 2, 1883
    d. Chicago, Ill., February 24, 1949
    U. S. Representative, 1921-23, 1925-27

GORSKI, Martin
    Democrat
    b. Poland, October 30, 1886
    d. Chicago, Ill., December 4, 1949
    U. S. Representative, December 4, 1949

GRAFF, Joseph Verdi
    Republican
    b. Terre Haute, Ind., July 1, 1854
    d. Peoria, Ill., November 10, 1921
    U. S. Representative, 1895-1911

GRAHAM, James McMahon
    Democrat
    b. Castleblayney, County Monaghan, Ireland, April
        14, 1852

d. Springfield, Ill., October 23, 1945
U. S. Representative, 1909-15

GRAHAM, William Johnson
    Republican
    b. near New Castle, Pa., February 7, 1872
    d. Washington, D. C., November 10, 1937
    U. S. Representative, 1917-24

GRANATA, Peter Charles
    Republican
    b. Chicago, Ill., October 28, 1898
    U. S. Representative, 1931-32

GRAY, Kenneth James
    Democrat
    b. West Frankfort, Ill., November 14, 1924
    U. S. Representative, 1955-

GREEN, Dwight D.
    b. Ligonier, Ind., January 9, 1897
    d. February 20, 1958
    Governor of Illinois, 1941-49

HADLEY, William Flavius Lester
    Republican
    b. near Collinsville, Ill., June 15, 1847
    d. Riverside, Calif., April 25, 1901
    U. S. Representative, 1895-97

HALL, Homer William
    Republican
    b. Shelbyville, Ill., July 22, 1870
    d. Bloomington, Ill., September 22, 1954
    U. S. Representative, 1927-33

HAMILTON, John M.
    b. Ridgewood, Ohio, May 28, 1847
    d. 1905
    Governor of Illinois, 1883-85

HARDIN, John J.
    Whig
    b. Frankfort, Ky., January 6, 1810
    d. at the Battle of Buena Vista, Mexico, February
        23, 1847
    U. S. Representative, 1843-45

HARDING, Abner Clark
    Republican
    b. East Hampton, Conn., February 10, 1807
    d. Monmouth, Ill., July 19, 1874
    U. S. Representative, 1865-69

HARRIS, Charles Murray
    Democrat
    b. Munfordsville, Ky., April 10, 1821
    d. Chicago, Ill., September 20, 1896
    U. S. Representative, 1863-65

HARRIS, Thomas Langnell
    Democrat
    b. Norwich, Conn., October 29, 1816
    d. Springfield, Ill., November 24, 1858
    U. S. Representative, 1849-51, 1855-58

HARRISON, Carter Henry
    Democrat
    b. near Lexington, Ky., February 15, 1825
    d. by assassination, Chicago, Ill., October 28,
       1893
    U. S. Representative, 1875-79

HARTZELL, William
    Democrat
    b. Canton, Ohio, February 20, 1837
    d. August 14, 1903
    U. S. Representative, 1875-79

HAWK, Robert Moffett Allison
    Republican
    b. near Rushville, Ind., April 23, 1839
    d. Washington, D. C., June 29, 1882
    U. S. Representative, 1879-82

HAWLEY, John Baldwin
    Republican
    b. Hawleyville, Conn., February 9, 1831
    d. Hot Springs, S. D., May 24, 1895
    U. S. Representative, 1869-75

HAY, John Breese
    Republican
    b. Belleville, Ill., January 8, 1834
    d. Belleville, Ill., June 16, 1916
    U. S. Representative, 1869-73

HAYES, Philip Cornelius
    Republican
    b. Granby, Conn., February 3, 1833
    d. Joliet, Ill., July 13, 1916
    U. S. Representative, 1877-81

HEIDINGER, James Vandaveer
    Republican
    b. near Mount Erie, Ill., July 17, 1882
    d. Phoenix, Ariz., March 22, 1945

U. S. Representative, 1941-45

HENDERSON, Thomas Jefferson
    Republican
    b. Brownsville, Tenn., November 29, 1824
    d. Washington, D. C., February 6, 1911
    U. S. Representative, 1875-95

HENRY, John
    Whig
    b. near Stanford, Ky., November 1, 1800
    d. St. Louis, Mo., April 28, 1882
    U. S. Representative, 1847

HILL, Charles Augustus
    Republican
    b. Truxton, N. Y., August 23, 1833
    d. Joliet, Ill., May 29, 1902
    U. S. Representative, 1889-91

HILL, Robert Potter
    Democrat (Illinois/Oklahoma)
    b. near Ewing, Ill., April 18, 1874
    d. Oklahoma City, Okla., October 29, 1937
    U. S. Representative, 1913-15 (Illinois), 1937 (Ok-
        lahoma)

HINEBAUGH, William Henry
    Progressive
    b. near Marshall, Mich., December 16, 1867
    d. Albion, Mich., September 22, 1943
    U. S. Representative, 1913-15

HINRICHSEN, William Henry
    Democrat
    b. Franklin, Ill., May 27, 1850
    d. Alexander, Ill., December 18, 1907
    U. S. Representative, 1897-99

HITT, Robert Roberts
    Republican
    b. Urbana, Ohio, January 16, 1834
    d. Narragansett Pier, R. I., September 19, 1906
    U. S. Representative, 1882-1906

HODGES, Charles Drury
    Democrat
    b. Queen Anne, Md., February 4, 1810
    d. Carrollton, Ill., April 1, 1884
    U. S. Representative, 1859

HOFFMAN, Elmer Joseph
    Republican

b. Du Page County near Wheaton, Ill., July 7, 1899
U. S. Representative, 1959-65

HOFFMAN, Richard William
    Republican
    b. Chicago, Ill., December 23, 1893
    U. S. Representative, 1949-57

HOGE, Joseph Pendleton
    Democrat
    b. Steubenville, Ohio, December 15, 1810
    d. San Francisco, Calif., August 14, 1891
    U. S. Representative, 1843-47

HOLADAY, William Perry
    Republican
    b. near Ridgefarm, Ill., December 14, 1882
    d. Georgetown, Ill., January 29, 1946
    U. S. Representative, 1923-33

HOPKINS, Albert Jarvis
    Republican
    b. near Cortland, Ill., August 15, 1846
    d. Aurora, Ill., August 23, 1922
    U. S. Representative, 1885-1903
    U. S. Senator, 1903-09

HORNER, Henry
    Democrat
    b. Chicago, Ill., November 30, 1878
    d. October 6, 1940
    Governor of Illinois, 1933-40

HOWELL, Evan (George)
    Republican
    b. Marion, Ill., September 21, 1905
    U. S. Representative, 1941-47

HOXWORTH, Stephen Arnold
    Democrat
    b. Maquon Township near Maquon, Ill., May 1, 1860
    d. Rapatee, Ill., January 25, 1930
    U. S. Representative, 1913-15

HUCK, Winnifred Sprague Mason
    b. Chicago, Ill., September 14, 1882
    d. Chicago, Ill., August 24, 1936
    U. S. Representative, 1922-23

HULL, Morton Dennison
    Republican
    b. Chicago, Ill., January 13, 1867
    d. Bennington, Vt., August 20, 1937

U. S. Representative, 1923-33

HULL, William Edgar
    Representative
    b. Lewiston, Ill., January 13, 1866
    d. Toronto, Canada, May 30, 1942
    U. S. Reprssentative, 1923-33

HUNTER, Andrew Jackson
    Democrat
    b. Greencastle, Ind., December 17, 1831
    d. Paris, Ill., January 12, 1913
    U. S. Representative, 1893-95, 1897-99

HURLBUT, Stephen Augustus
    Republican
    b. Charleston, S. C., November 29, 1815
    d. Lima, Peru, March 27, 1882
    U. S. Representative, 1873-77

IGOE, James Thomas
    Democrat
    b. Chicago, Ill., October 23, 1883
    U. S. Representative, 1927-33

IGOE, Michael Lambert
    Democrat
    b. St. Paul, Minn., April 16, 1885
    d. Chicago, Ill., August 21, 1967
    U. S. Representative, 1935

INGERSOLL, Eban Clark
    Republican
    b. Dresden, N. Y., December 12, 1831
    d. Washington, D. C., May 31, 1879
    U. S. Representative, 1864-71

IRELAND, Clifford Cady
    Republican
    b. Washburn, Ill., February 14, 1878
    d. Chicago, Ill., May 24, 1930
    U. S. Representative, 1917-23

JENISON, Edward Halsey
    Republican
    b. Fond du Lac, Wis., July 27, 1907
    U. S. Representative, 1947-53

JETT, Thomas Marion
    Democrat
    b. near Greenville, Ill., May 1, 1862
    d. Litchfield, Ill., January 10, 1939
    U. S. Representative, 1897-1903

JOHNSON, Anton Joseph
    Republican
    b. Peoria, Ill., October 20, 1878
    d. Macomb, Ill., April 16, 1958
    U. S. Representative, 1939-49

JOHNSON, Calvin Dean
    Republican
    b. Fordville, Ky., November 22, 1898
    U. S. Representative, 1943-45

JOHNSON, William Richard
    Republican
    b. Rock Island, Ill., May 15, 1875
    d. Freeport, Ill., January 2, 1938
    U. S. Representative, 1925-33

JONAS, Edgar Allan
    Republican
    b. Mishicot, Wis., October 14, 1885
    d. Evanston, Ill., November 14, 1965
    U. S. Representative, 1949-55

JUDD, Normal Buel
    b. Rome, N. Y., January 10, 1815
    d. Chicago, Ill., November 10, 1878
    U. S. Representative, 1867-71

JUUL, Niels
    Republican
    b. Randers, Denmark, April 27, 1859
    d. Chicago, Ill., December 4, 1929
    U. S. Representative, 1917-21

KANE, Elias Kent
    Democrat
    b. New York, N. Y., June 7, 1794
    d. Washington, D. C., December 12, 1835
    U. S. Senator, 1825-35

KARCH, Charles Adam
    Democrat
    b. Engleman Township, Ill., March 17, 1875
    d. St. Louis, Mo., November 6, 1932
    U. S. Representative, 1931-32

KEENEY, Russell Watson
    Republican
    b. Pittsfield, Ill., December 29, 1897
    d. Bethesda, Md., January 11, 1958
    U. S. Representative, 1957-58

KELLER, Kent Ellsworth
    Democrat
    b. near Campbell Hill, Ill., June 4, 1867
    d. Ava, Ill., September 3, 1954
    U. S. Representative, 1931-41

KELLOGG, William
    Republican
    b. Kelloggsville, Ohio, July 8, 1814
    d. Peoria, Ill., December 20, 1872
    U. S. Representative, 1857-63

KELLY, Edward Austin
    Democrat
    b. Chicago, Ill., April 3, 1892
    d. Chicago, Ill., August 30, 1969
    U. S. Representative, 1931-43, 1945-47

KERN, Frederick John
    Democrat
    b. near Millstadt, Ill., September 6, 1864
    d. Belleville, Ill., November 9, 1931
    U. S. Representative, 1901-03

KERNER, Otto
    b. Chicago, Ill., August 15, 1908
    d. May 9, 1976
    Governor of Illinois, 1961-68

KING, Edward John
    Republican
    b. Springfield, Mass., July 1, 1867
    d. Washington, D. C., February 17, 1929
    U. S. Representative, 1915-1929

KLUCZYNSKI, John Carl
    Democrat
    b. Chicago, Ill., February 15, 1896
    U. S. Representative, 1951-

KNAPP, Anthony Lousett
    Democrat
    b. Middleton, N. Y., June 14, 1828
    d. Springfield, Ill., May 24, 1881
    U. S. Representative, 1861-65

KNAPP. Robert McCarty
    Democrat
    b. New York, N. Y., April 21, 1831
    d. Jerseyville, Ill., June 24, 1889
    U. S. Representative, 1873-75, 1877-79

KNOPF, Philip
    Republican
    b. Long Grove, Ill., November 18, 1847
    d. Chicago, Ill., August 14, 1920
    U. S. Representative, 1903-09

KNOX, James
    Whig
    b. Canajoharie, N. Y., July 4, 1807
    d. Knoxville, Ill., October 8, 1876
    U. S. Representative, 1853-57

KOCIALKOWSKI, Leo Paul
    Democrat
    b. Chicago, Ill., August 16, 1882
    d. Chicago, Ill., September 27, 1958
    U. S. Representative, 1933-43

KUNZ, Stanley Henry
    Democrat
    b. Nanticoke, Pa.. September 26, 1864
    d. Chicago, Ill., April 23, 1946
    U. S. Representative, 1921-31, 1932-33

KUYKENDALL, Andrew Jackson
    Republican
    b. Gallatin County, Ill., March 3, 1815
    d. Vienna, Ill., May 11, 1891
    U. S. Representative, 1865-67

LANDES, Silas Zephaniah
    Democrat
    b. Augusta County, Va., May 15, 1842
    d. Mount Carmel, Ill., May 23, 1910
    U. S. Representative, 1885-59

LANE, Edward
    Democrat
    b. Cleveland, Ohio, March 27, 1842
    d. Hillsboro, Ill., October 30, 1912
    U. S. Representative, 1887-95

LATHORP, William
    Republican
    b. near Le Roy, N. Y., April 17, 1825
    d. Rockford, Ill., November 19, 1907
    U. S. Representative, 1877-79

LAWLER, Frank
    b. Rochester, Ill., June 25, 1842
    d. Chicago, Ill., January 17, 1896
    U. S. Representative, 1885-91

LE MOYNE, John Valcoulon
    Democrat
    b. Washington, Pa., November 17, 1828
    d. Baltimore, Md., July 27, 1918
    U. S. Representative, 1876-77

LEWIS, James Hamilton
    Democrat (Washington/Illinois)
    b. Danville, Va., May 18, 1863
    d. Washington, D. C., April 9, 1939
    U. S. Representative, 1897-99 (Washington)
    U. S. Senator, 1913-19, 1931-39 (Illinois)

LEWIS, John Henry
    Republican
    b. near Ithaca, N. Y., July 21, 1830
    d. Knoxville, Ill., January 9, 1929
    U. S. Representative, 1881-83

LIBORATI, Roland Victor
    Democrat
    b. Chicago, Ill., December 29, 1900
    U. S. Representative 1957-65

LINCOLN, Abraham
    Whig
    b. Hardin County, Ky., February 12, 1809
    d. by assassination, Washington, D. C., April 14,
        1865
    U. S. Representative, 1847-49
    16th President of the United States, 1861-65

LINEHAN, Neil Joseph
    Democrat
    b. Chicago, Ill., September 23, 1895
    d. Chicago, Ill., August 23, 1967
    U. S. Representative, 1949-51

LINK, William Walter
    Democrat
    b. Swiec, Poland, February 12, 1884
    d. Chicago, Ill., September 23, 1950
    U. S. Representatibe, 1945-47

LOGAN, John Alexander
    Republican
    b. Murphysboro, Ill., February 9, 1826
    d. Washington, D. C., December 29, 1886
    U. S. Representative, 1859-62 (Democrat), 1867-71
        (Republican)
    U. S. Senator, 1871-77, 1879-86

LONG, Lewis Marshall
    Democrat
    b. Gardner, Ill., June 22, 1883
    d. Sandwich, Ill., September 9, 1957
    U. S. Representative, 1937-39

LORIMER, William
    Republican
    b. Manchester, England, April 27, 1861
    d. Chicago, Ill., September 13, 1934
    U. S. Representative, 1895-1901, 1903-09
    U. S. Senator, 1909-12

LOVEJOY, Owen
    Republican
    b. Albion, Me., January 6, 1811
    d. Brooklyn, N. Y., March 25, 1864
    U. S. Representative, 1857-64

LOWDEN, Frank Orren
    Republican
    b. Sunrise, Minn., January 26, 1861
    d. Tuscon, Ariz., March 20, 1943
    U. S. Representative, 1906-11
    Governor of Illinois, 1917-21

LUCAS, Scott Wike
    Democrat
    b. near Chandlerville, Ill., February 19, 1892
    d. Rocky Mount, N. C., February 22, 1968
    U. S. Representative, 1935-39
    U. S. Senator, 1939-51

LUNDIN, Frederick
    Republican
    b. in parish of Vestra Tollstad, Hastholem, Sweden,
        May 18, 1868
    d. Beverly Hills, Calif., August 20, 1947
    U. S. Representative, 1909-11

MACIEJEWSKI, Anton Frank
    Democrat
    b. Anderson, Tex., January 3, 1893
    d. Chicago, Ill., September 25, 1949
    U. S. Representative, 1939-42

MACK, Peter Francis, Jr.
    Democrat
    b. Carlinville, Ill., November 1, 1916
    U. S. Representative, 1949-63

MADDEN, Martin Barnaby
    Republican

d. Washington, D. C., February 25, 1925
U. S. Representative, 1917-19
U. S. Senator, 1919-25

MCCORMICK, Ruth Hanna
Republican
b. Cleveland, Ohio, March 27, 1880
d. Chicago, Ill., December 31, 1944
U. S. Representative, 1929-31

MCDANNOLD, John James
Democrat
b. Mount Sterling, Ill., August 29, 1851
d. Chicago, Ill., February 3, 1904
U. S. Representative, 1893-95

MCDERMOTT, James Thomas
Democrat
b. Grand Rapids, Mich., February 13, 1872
d. Chicago, Ill., February 7, 1938
U. S. Representative, 1907-14, 1915-17

MCGANN, Lawrence Edward
Democrat
b. Galway, Ireland, February 2, 1852
d. Oak Park, Ill., July 22, 1928
U. S. Representative, 1891-1895

MCGAVIN, Charles
Republican
b. Riverton, Ill., January 10, 1874
d. Chicago, Ill., December 17, 1940
U. S. Representative, 1905-09

MCKENZIE, John Charles
Republican
b. near Elizabeth, Woodbine Township, Ill.,
      February 18, 1860
d. Elizabeth, Ill., September 17, 1941
U. S. Representative, 1911-25

MCKEOUGH, Raymond Stephen
b. Chicago, Ill., April 29, 1888
U. S. Representative, 1935-43

MCKINLEY, William Brown
b. Petersburg, Ill., September 5, 1856
d. Martinsville, Ind., December 7, 1926
U. S. Representative, 1905-13, 1915-21
U. S. Senator, 1921-26

MCKINNEY, James
Republican
b. Oquawka, Ill., April 14, 1852

d. Aledo, Ill., September 29, 1934
U. S. Representative, 1905-13

MCLEAN, John
b. near Guilford Court House (now Greensboro),
   N. C., February 4, 1791
d. Shawneetown, Ill., October 13, 1830
U. S. Representative, 1818-19
U. S. Senator, 1824-25, 1829-30

MCLOSKEY, Robert Thaddeus
Republican
b. Monmouth, Ill., June 26, 1907
U. S. Representative, 1963-65

MCMILLEN, Rolla Coral
Republican
b. near Monticello, Ill., October 5, 1880
d. Evanston, Ill., May 6, 1961
U. S. Representative, 1944-51

MCNEELY, Thompson Ware
Democrat
b. Jacksonville, Ill., October 5, 1835
d. Petersburg, Ill., July 23, 1921
U. S. Representative, 1869-73

MCNULTA, John
Republican
b. New York, N. Y., November 9, 1837
d. Washington, D. C., February 22, 1900
U. S. Representative, 1873-75

MCROBERTS, Samuel
Democrat
b. near Maeystown, Ill., April 12, 1799
d. Cincinnati, Ohio, March 27, 1843
U. S. Senator, 1841-43

MCVEY, William Estus
Republican
b. near Lee's Creek, Ohio, December 13, 1885
d. Washington, D. C., August 10, 1958
U. S. Representative, 1951- 58

MEEKS, James Andrew
Democrat
Democrat
b. New Matamoras, Ohio, March 7, 1864
d. Danville, Ill., November 10, 1946
U. S. Representative, 1933-39

METCALFE, Ralph H.
    Democrat
    b. May 29, 1910
    U. S. Representative, 1971-

MICHAELSON, Mayne Alfred
    Republican
    b. Kristiansand, Norway, September 7, 1878
    d. Chicago, Ill., October 26, 1949
    U. S. Representative, 1921-31

MICHALEK, Anthony
    Republican
    b. Radvanov, Bohemia, January 16, 1878
    d. Chicago, Ill., December 21, 1916
    U. S. Representative, 1905-07

MICHEL, Robert Henry
    Republican
    b. Peoria, Ill., March 5, 1923
    U. S. Representative, 1957-

MICKEY, J. Ross
    Democrat
    b. Eldorado Township, Ill., January 5, 1856
    d. Excelsior Springs, Mo., March 20, 1928

MIKVA, Abner J.
    Democrat
    b. Milwaukee, Wis., January 21, 1926
    U. S. Representative, 1969-

MILLER, Edward Edwin
    Republican
    b. Creston, Iowa, July 22, 1880
    d. St. Louis, Mo., August 1, 1946
    U. S. Representative, 1923-25

MILLS, Daniel Webster
    Republican
    b. Waynesville, Ohio, February 25, 1838
    d. December 16, 1904
    U. S. Representative, 1897-99

MITCHELL, Arthur Wergs
    Democrat
    b. near Lafayette, Ala., December 22, 1883
    d. near Petersburg, Va., May 9, 1968
    U. S. Representative, 1935-43

MOLONY, Richard Sheppard
    b. Northfield, N. H., June 28, 1811
    d. Humboldt, Neb., December 14, 1891

U. S. Representative, 1851-53

MOORE, Allen Francis
      Republican
      b. St. Charles, Ill., September 30, 1869
      d. San Antonio, Tex., August 18, 1945
      U. S. Representative, 1921-25

MOORE, Jesse Hale
      Republican
      b. near Lebanon, Ill., April 22, 1817
      d. Callao, Peru, July 11, 1883
      U. S. Representative, 1869-73

MORRIS, Isaac Newton
      Democrat
      b. Bethel, Ohio, January 22, 1812
      d. Quincy, Ill., October 29, 1879
      U. S. Representative, 1857-61

MORRISON, John Alexander
      Democrat
      b. Colerain, Pa., April 12, 1816
      d. Cochranville, Pa., August 14, 1888
      U. S. Representative, 1856-57

MORRISON, William Ra;;s
      Democrat
      b. Prairie du Long, near present town of Waterloo,
            Ill., September 14, 1825
      d. Waterloo, Ill., September 29, 1909
      U. S. Representative, 1863-65, 1873-87

MOULTON, Samuel Wheeler
      Democrat
      b. Wenham, Mass., January 20, 1821
      d. Shelbyville, Ill., June 3, 1905
      U. S. Representative, 1865-67, 1881-85

MOSLEY, William James
      Republican
      b. County Cork, Ireland, May 22, 1851
      d. Delavan Lake near Delavan, Wis., August 4,
            1938
      U. S. Representative, 1909-11

MOYNIHAN, Patrick Henry
      Republican
      b. Chicago, Ill., September 25, 1869
      d. Chicago, Ill., May 20, 1946
      U. S. Representative, 1933-35

MURPHY, Everett Jerome
    Republican
    b. Nashville, Ill., July 14, 1852
    d. Joliet, Ill., April 10, 1922
    U. S. Representative, 1895-97

MURPHY, Morgan F., Jr.
    Democrat
    b. April 16, 1932
    U. S. Representative, 1971-

MURPHY, William Thomas
    Democrat
    b. Chicago, Ill., August 7, 1899
    U. S. Representative, 1959-71

MURRAY, James Cunningham
    Democrat
    b. Chicago, Ill., May 16, 1917
    U. S. Representative, 1955-57

NEECE, William Henry
    Democrat
    b. near Springfield, Ill., February 26, 1831
    d. Chicago, Ill., January 3, 1909
    U. S. Representative, 1883-87

NESBIT, Walter
    Democrat
    b. Belleville, Ill., May 1, 1878
    d. Belleville, Ill., December 6, 1938
    U. S. Representative, 1933-35

NEWBERRY, Walter Cass
    Democrat
    b. Sangerfield, N. Y., December 23, 1835
    d. Chicago, Ill., July 20, 1912
    U. S. Representative, 1891-93

NOONAN, Edward Thomas
    Democrat
    b. Macomb, Ill., October 23, 1861
    d. Chicago, Ill., December 19, 1923
    U. S. Representative, 1899-1901

NORTON, Jesse Olds
    Republican
    b. Bennington, Vt., December 25, 1812
    d. Chicago, Ill., August 3, 1875
    U. S. Representative, 1853-57, 1863-65

O'BRIEN, Thomas Joseph
    Democrat

b. Chicago, Ill., April 30, 1878
d. Bethesda, Md., April 14, 1964
U. S. Representative, 1933-39, 1943-64

OGILVIE, Richard B.
    Republican
    b. Kansas City, Mo., February 22, 1923
    Governor of Illinois, 1969-73

OGLESBY, Richard James
    Republican
    b. Floydsburg, Ky., July 25, 1824
    d. Elkhart, Ill., April 24, 1884
    Governor of Illinois, 1865-69, 1873
    U. S. Senator, 1873-79
    Governor of Illinois, 1885-89

O'HAIR, Frank Trimble
    Democrat
    b. near Paris, Ill., March 12, 1870
    d. Paris, Ill., August 3, 1932
    U. S. Representative, 1913-15

O'HARA, Barratt
    Democrat
    b. Saint Joseph, Mich., April 28, 1882
    d. Washington, D. C., August 11, 1969
    U. S. Representative, 1949-51, 1953-69

OWENS, Thomas Leonard
    Republican
    b. Chicago, Ill., December 21, 1897
    d. Bethesda, Md., June 7, 1948
    U. S. Representative, 1947-48

PADDOCK, George Arthur
    Republican
    b. Winnetka, Ill., March 24, 1885
    d. Evanston, Ill., December 29, 1964
    U. S. Representative, 1941-43

PALMER, John McAuley
    Democrat
    b. Eagle Creek, Ky., September 13, 1817
    d. Springfield, Ill., September 25, 1900
    Governor of Illinois (Republican), 1869-73
    U. S. Senator, 1891-97

PARSONS, Claude VanCleve
    Democrat
    b. near McCormick, Ill., October 7, 1895
    d. Washington, D. C., May 23, 1941
    U. S. Representative, 1930-41

PAYSON, Lewis Edwin
      Republican
      b. Providence, R. I., September 17, 1840
      d. Washington, D. C., October 4, 1909
      U. S. Representative, 1881-91

PERCY, Charles Harting
      Republican
      b. Pensacola, Fla., September 27, 1919
      U. S. Senator, 1967-

PLUMB, Ralph
      Republican
      b. Busti, N. Y., May 29, 1816
      d. Strator, Ill., April 8, 1903
      U. S. Representative, 1885-89

POPE, Nathaniel
      b. Louisville, Ky., January 5, 1784
      d. St. Louis, Mo., January 22, 1850
      U. S. Representative (Territorial Delegate), 1816-
         1818

POST, Philip Sidney
      Republican
      b. Florida, N. Y., March 19, 1833
      d. Washington, D. C., January 6, 1895
      U. S. Representative, 1887-95

PRICE, Charles Melvin
      Democrat
      b. East St. Louis, Ill., January 1, 1905
      U. S. Representative, 1945-

PRINCE, George Washington
      Republican
      b. Tazewell County, Illinois, March 4, 1854
      d. Los Angeles, Calif., September 26, 1939
      U. S. Representative, 1895-1913

PUCINSKI, Roman Conrad
      Democrat
      b. Buffalo, N. Y., May 13, 1919
      U. S. Representative, 1959-

RAILSBACK, Thomas F.
      Republican
      b. Moline, Ill., January 22, 1932
      U. S. Representative, 1967-

RAINEY, Henry Thomas
      Democrat
      b. Carrollton, Ill., August 20, 1860

d. St. Louis, Mo., August 14, 1934
U. S. Representative, 1903-21, 1923-34
    Speaker, 1933-34

RAINEY, John William
    Democrat
    b. Chicago, Ill., December 21, 1880
    d. Chicago, Ill., May 4, 1923
    U. S. Representative, 1918-23

RAMEY, Frank Marion
    Republican
    b. Hillsboro, Ill., September 23, 1881
    d. Hillsboro, Ill., March 27, 1942
    U. S. Representative, 1929-31

RATHBONE, Henry Riggs
    Republican
    b. Washington, D. C., February 12, 1870
    d. Chicago, Ill., July 15, 1928
    U. S. Representative, 1923-28

RAUM, Green Berry
    Republican
    b. Golconda, Ill., December 3, 1829
    d. Chicago, Ill., December 18, 1909
    U. S. Representative, 1867-69

RAY, William Henry
    Republican
    b. Amenia, N. Y., December 14, 1812
    d. Rushville, Ill., January 25, 1881
    U. S. Representative, 1873-75

REED, Chauncey William
    Republican
    b. West Chicago, Ill., June 2, 1890
    d. Bethesda, Md., February 9, 1956
    U. S. Representative, 1935-56

REEVES, Walter
    Republican
    b. near Brownsville, Pa., September 25, 1848
    d. Streator, Ill., April 9, 1909
    U. S. Representative, 1895-1903

REID, Charlotte Thompson
    Republican
    b. Kankakee, Ill., September 27, 1913
    U. S. Representative, 1963-71
    Member Federal Communications Commission, 1971-

REID, Frank R.
    Republican
    b. Aurora, Ill., August 18, 1879
    d. Aurora, Ill., January 25, 1945
    U. S. Representative, 1923-35

REMANN, Frederick
    b. Vandalia, Ill., March 10, 1847
    d. Vandalia, Ill., July 14, 1895
    U. S. Representative, 1895

RESA, Alexander John
    Democrat
    b. Chicago, Ill., August 4, 1887
    d. Evanston, Ill., July 4, 1964
    U. S. Representative, 1945-47

REYNOLDS, John
    Democrat
    b. Montgomery County near Philadelphia, Pa., Feb-
        ruary 26, 1789
    d. Belleville, Ill., May 8, 1865
    Governor of Illinois, 1830-34
    U. S. Representative, 1834-37, 39-43

RICE, Edward Young
    Democrat
    b. near Russellville, Ky., February 8, 1820
    d. Hillsboro, Ill., April 16, 1883
    U. S. Representative, 1871-73

RICE, John Blake
    Republican
    b. Easton, Md., May 28, 1809
    d. Norfolk, Va., December 17, 1874
    U. S. Representative, 1873-74

RICHARDSON, William Alexander
    Democrat
    b. near Lexington, Ky., January 16, 1811
    d. Quincy, Ill., December 27, 1875
    U. S. Representative, 1847-56, 1861-63
    U. S. Senator, 1863-65

RIGGS, James Milton
    Democrat
    b. near Winchester, Ill., April 17, 1839
    d. Winchester, Ill., November 18, 1933
    U. S. Representative, 1883-87

RIGNEY, Hugh McPheeters
    Democrat
    b. Arthur, Ill., July 31, 1873

d. Springfield, Ill., October 12, 1950
U. S. Representative, 1937-39

RINAKER, John Irving
    Republican
    b. Baltimore, Md., November 1, 1830
    d. Eustis, Fla., January 15, 1915
    U. S. Representative, 1896-97

RIVES, Zeno John
    Republican
    b. near Greenfield, Ind., February 22, 1874
    d. Decatur, Ill., September 2, 1939
    U. S. Representative, 1905-07

ROBINSON, James Carroll
    Democrat
    b. near Paris, Ill., August 19, 1823
    d. Springfield, Ill., November 3, 1886
    U. S. Representative, 1859-65, 1871-75

ROBINSON, John McCracken
    Democrat
    b. near Georgetown, Ky., April 10, 1794
    d. Ottawa, Ill., April 25, 1843
    U. S. Senator, 1830-34

RODENBERG, William August
    Republican
    b. Chester, Ill., October 30, 1865
    d. Washington, D. C., September 10, 1937
    U. S. Representative, 1899-1901, 1901-13, 1915-23

RONAN, Daniel John
    Democrat
    b. Chicago, Ill., July 23, 1914
    d. Chicago, Ill., August 13, 1969
    U. S. Representative, 1965-69

ROSS, Lewis Winans
    Democrat
    b. near Seneca Falls, N. Y., December 8, 1812
    d. Lewiston, Ill., October 20, 1895
    U. S. Representative, 1863-69

ROSTENKOWSKI, Daniel David (Dan)
    Democrat
    b. Chicago, Ill., January 2, 1928
    U. S. Representative, 1959-

ROWAN, William A.
    Democrat
    b. Chicago, Ill., November 24, 1882

d. Chicago, Ill., May 31, 1961
U. S. Representative, 1943-47

ROWELL, Jonathan Harvey
    Republican
    b. Haverhill, N. H., February 10, 1833
    d. Bloomington, Ill., May 15, 1908
    U. S. Representative, 1883-91

SABATH, Adolph Joachim
    Democrat
    b. Zabori, Czechoslovakia, April 4, 1866
    d. Bethesda, Md., November 6, 1952
    U. S. Representative, 1907-52

SCHAEFER, Edwin Martin
    Democrat
    b. Belleville, Ill., May 14, 1887
    d. St. Louis, Mo., November 8, 1950
    U. S. Representative, 1933-43

SCHISLER, Darwin Gale
    Democrat
    b. Indian Point Township, Ill., March 2, 1933
    U. S. Representative, 1965-67

SCHUETZ, Leonard William
    Democrat
    b. Posen, Germany (later Poland), November 16,
       1887
    d. Washington, D. C., February 13, 1944
    U. S. Representative, 1931-44

SCOTT, Owen
    b. Jackson Township, Ill., July 6, 1848
    d. Decatur, Ill., December 21, 1928
    U. S. Representative, 1891-93

SELBY, Thomas Jefferson
    Democrat
    b. Delaware County, Ohio, December 4, 1840
    d. Hardin, Ill., March 10, 1917
    U. S. Representative, 1901-03

SEMPLE, James
    Democrat
    b. Green County, Ky., January 5, 1798
    d. Elsah, Ill., December 20, 1866
    U. S. Senator, 1843-47

SHAPIRO, Samuel H.
    Democrat
    b. April 25, 1907

Governor of Illinois, 1968-69

SHAW, Aaron
    Democrat
    b. near Goshen, N. Y., December 19, 1811
    d. Olney, Ill., January 7, 1887
    U. S. Representative, 1857-59, 1883-85

SHAW, Guy Loren
    Republican
    b. near Summer Hill, Ill., May 10, 1881
    d. Normal, Ill., May 19, 1950
    U. S. Representative, 1921-23

SHEEHAN, Timothy Patrick
    Republican
    b. Chicago, Ill., February 21, 1909
    U. S. Representative, 1951-59

SHERMAN, Lawrence Yates
    Republican
    b. near Piqua, Ohio, November 8, 1858
    d. Daytona Beach, Fla., September 15, 1939
    U. S. Senator, March 26, 1913-21

SHERWIN, John Crocker
    Republican
    b. Gouverneur, N. Y., February 8, 1838
    d. Benton Harbor, Mich., January 1, 1904
    U. S. Representative, 1879-83

SHIELDS, James
    Democrat (Illinois/Minnesota/Missouri)
    b. Altmore, County Tyrone, Ireland, May 10, 1810
    d. Ottumwa, Iowa, June 11, 1879
    U. S. Senator, 1849, 1849-55 (Illinois)
        1858-59 (Minnesota)
        1879 (Missouri)

SHIPLEY, George Edward
    Democrat
    b. Richland County near Olney, Ill., April 21,
        1927
    U. S. Representative, 1959-

SIMPSON, Edna Oakes
    Republican
    b. Carrollton, Ill., October 28, 1891
    U. S. Representative, 1959-61

SIMPSON, James, Jr.
    Republican
    b. Chicago, January 7, 1905

   d. Wadsworth, Ill., February 29, 1960
   U. S. Representative, 1933-35

SIMPSON, Sidney Elmer (Sid)
   b. Carrollton, Ill., September 20, 1894
   d. Pittsfield, Ill., October 26, 1958
   U. S. Representative, 1943-58

SINGLETON, James Washington
   Democrat
   b. Paxton, Va., November 23, 1811
   d. near Quincy, Ill., April 4, 1892
   U. S. Representative, 1879-83

SLADE, Charles
   Democrat
   b. England, ---
   d. near Vincennes, Ind., July 26, 1834
   U. S. Representative, 1833-34

SLATTERY, James Michael
   Democrat
   b. Chicago, Ill., July 29, 1878
   d. Lake Geneva, Wis., August 28, 1948
   U. S. Senator, 1939-40

SMALL, Len
   Republican
   b. Kankakee, Ill., June 16, 1862
   d. May 17, 1936
   Governor of Illinois, 1921-29

SMITH, Dietrich Conrad
   Republican
   b. Ost Friesland, Hanover, Germany, April 4,
      1840
   d. Pekin, Ill., April 18, 1914
   U. S. Representative, 1881-83

SMITH, Frank Leslie
   Republican
   b. Dwight, Ill., November 24, 1867
   d. Dwight, Ill., August 30, 1950
   U. S. Representative, 1919-21
   U. S. Senator, 1926-28

SMITH, George Washington
   Republican
   b. Putnam County, Ohio, August 18, 1846
   d. Murphysboro, Ill., November 30, 1907
   U. S. Representative, 1889-1907

SMITH, Ralph Tyler
    Republican
    b. Granite City, Ill., October 6, 1915
    U. S. Senator, 1969-70

SMITH, Robert
    Democrat
    b. Petersborough, N. H., June 12, 1802
    d. Alton, Ill., December 21, 1867
    U. S. Representative, 1843-49, 1857-59

SMITH, Thomas Vernor
    Democrat
    b. Blanket, Tex., April 26, 1890
    d. Hyattsville, Md., May 24, 1964
    U. S. Representative, 1939-41

SNAPP, Henry
    Republican
    b. Livonia, N. Y., June 30, 1822
    d. Joliet, Ill., November 26, 1895
    U. S. Representative, 1871-73

SNAPP, Howard Malcolm
    Republican
    b. Joliet, Ill., September 27, 1855
    d. Joliet, Ill., August 14, 1938
    U. S. Representative, 1903-11

SNOW, Herman Wilber
    Democrat
    b. Michigan City, Ind., July 3, 1836
    d. Kankakee, Ill., August 25, 1914
    U. S. Representative, 1891-93

SNYDER, Adam Wilson
    Van Buren Democrat
    b. Connesville, Pa., October 6, 1799
    d. Belleville, Ill., May 14, .842
    U. S. Representative, 1837-39

SPARKS, William Andrew Jackson
    Democrat
    b. near New Albany, Ind., November 19, 1828
    d. St. Louis, Mo., May 7, 1904
    U. S. Representative, 1876-83

SPRINGER, William Lee
    Republican
    b. Sullivan, Ind., April 12, 1909
    U. S. Representative, 1951-

SPRINGER, William McKendree
    Democrat
    b. near New Lebanon, Ind., May 30, 1836
    d. Washington, D. C., December 4, 1903
    U. S. Representative, 1875-95

SPROUL, Elliott Wilford
    Republican
    b. Apohaqui, New Brunswick, Canada, December 28,
        1856
    d. Chicago, Ill., June 22, 1935
    U. S. Representative, 1921-31

STACK, Edmund John
    Democrat
    b. Chicago, Ill., January 31, 1874
    d. Chicago, Ill., April 12, 1957
    U. S. Representative, 1911-13

STELLE, John H.
    Democrat
    Governor of Illinois, 1940-41

STEPHENSON, Benjamin
    Democrat
    b. Kentucky, ---
    d. Edwardsville, Ill., October 10, 1822
    U. S. Representative (Territorial Delegate, 1814-
        16)

STERLING, John Allen
    Republican
    b. near Le Roy, Ill., February 1, 1857
    d. near Pontiac, Ill., October 17, 1918
    U. S. Representative, 1903-14, 1915-18

STEVENS, Bradford Newcomb
    Democrat
    b. Boscawen, N. H., January 3, 1813
    d. Tiskilwa, Ill., November 10, 1885
    U. S. Representative, 1871-73

STEVENSON, Adlai Ewing
    Democrat
    b. Christian County, Ky., October 23, 1835
    d. Chicago, Ill., June 14, 1914
    U. S. Representative, 1875-77, 1879-81
    Vice President of the United States, 1893-97

STEVENSON, Adlai E.
    Democrat
    b. Los Angeles, Calif., February 5, 1900
    d. Chicago, Ill., July 14, 1965

Governor of Illinois, 1949-53
U. S. Ambassador to the United Nations, 1961-65

STEVENSON, Adlai Ewing III
    Democrat
    b. Chicago, Ill., October 10, 1930
    U. S. Senator, 1970-

STEWARD, Lewis
    Democrat
    b. near Hollisterville, Pa., November 21, 1824
    d. Pianio, Ill., August 27, 1896
    U. S. Representative, 1891-93

STONE, Claudius Ulysses
    Democrat
    b. Menard County near Greenville, Illinois, May
        11, 1879
    d. Peoria, Ill., November 13, 1957
    U. S. Representative, 1911-17

STRATTON, William Grant
    Republican
    b. Ingleside, Ill., February 26, 1914
    U. S. Representative, 1941-43, 1947-49
    Governor of Illinois, 1953-61

STRINGER, Lawrence Beaumont
    Democrat
    b. near Atlantic City, N. J., February 24, 1866
    d. Lincoln, Ill., December 5, 1942
    U. S. Representative, 1913-15

STUART, John Todd
    Democrat
    b. near Lexington, Ky., November 10, 1807
    d. Springfield, Ill., November 23, 1885
    U. S. Representative, 1839-43 (Whig), 1863-65
        (Democrat)

SUMNER, Jesse
    Republican
    b. Milford, Ill., July 17, 1898
    U. S. Representative, 1939-47

TANNER, John R.
    Republican
    b. Warrick County, Ind., April 4, 1844
    d. 1901
    Governor of Illinois, 1897-1901

TAVENNER, Clyde Howard
    Democrat

b. Cordova, Ill., February 4, 1882
d. Washington, D. C., February 6, 1942
U. S. Representative, 1913-17

TAYLOR, Abner
    Republican
    b. Bangor, Me., 1829
    d. Washington, D. C., April 13, 1903
    U. S. Representative, 1889-93

THISTLEWOOD, Napoleon Bonaparte
    Republican
    b. near Harrington, Del., March 30, 1837
    d. Cairo, Ill., September 15, 1915
    U. S. Representative. 1908-13

THOMAS, Jesse Burgess
    Whig (Indiana/Illinois)
    b. Elizabethtown (now Hagerstown), Md., 1777
    d. Mount Vernon, Ohio, May 4, 1853
    U. S. Representative (Territorial Delegate),
        1808-09 (Indiana)
    U. S. Senator, 1818-29 (Illinois)

THOMAS, John Robert
    Republican
    b. Mount Vernon, Ill., October 11, 1846
    d. McAlester, Okla., January 19, 1914
    U. S. Representative, 1879-89

THOMPSON, Chester Charles
    Democrat
    b. Rock Island, Ill., September 19, 1893
    d. Rock Island, Ill., January 30, 1971
    U. S. Representative, 1933-39

THOMSON, Charles Marsh
    People's Party
    b. Chicago, Ill., February 1788
    d. Chicago, Ill., August 2, 1848
    U. S. Representative, 1824-26

THORNTON, Anthony
    Democrat
    b. near Paris, Ky., November 9, 1814
    d. Shelbyville, Ill., September 10, 1904
    U. S. Representative, 1865-67

TIPTON, Thomas Foster
    Republican
    b. near Harrisburg, Ohio, August 29, 1833
    d. Bloomington, Ill., February 7, 1904
    U. S. Representative, 1877-79

TOWNSHEND, Richard Wellington
    Democrat
    b. near Upper Marboro, Md., April 30, 1840
    d. Washington, D. C., March 9, 1889
    U. S. Representative, 1877-89

TRUMBULL, Lyman
    Republican
    b. Colchester, Conn., October 12, 1813
    d. Chicago, Ill., June 25, 1896
    U. S. Senator, 1855-73

TURNER, Thomas Johnston
    Democrat
    b. Trumbull County, Ohio, April 5, 1815
    d. Hot Springs, Ark., April 4, 1874
    U. S. Representative, 1847-49

TWYMAN, Robert Joseph
    Republican
    b. Indianapolis, Ind., June 18, 1897
    U. S. Representative, 1947-49

VAIL, Richard Bernard
    Republican
    b. Chicago, Ill., August 31, 1895
    d. Chicago, Ill., July 29, 1955
    U. S. Representative, 1947-49, 1951-53

VELDE, Harold Himmel
    Republican
    b. near Parkland, Ill., April 1, 1910
    U. S. Representative, 1949-57

VURSELL, Charles Wesley
    Republican
    b. Salem, Ill., February 8, 1881
    U. S. Representative, 1943-59

WALKER, Daniel
    Democrat
    b. Washington, D. C., August 6, 1922
    Governor of Illinois, 1973-

WARD, James Hugh
    Democrat
    b. Chicago, Ill., November 30, 1853
    d. Chicago, Ill., August 15, 1916
    U. S. Representatibe, 1885-87

WARD, Jasper Delos
    Republican
    b. Java, N. Y., February 1, 1829

d. Denver, Colo., August 6, 1902
U. S. Representative, 1873-75

WARNER, Vespasian
    Republican
    b. Mount Pleasant (now Farmer City), Ill., April
        23, 1842
    d. Clinton, Ill., March 31, 1925
    U. S. Representative, 1895-1905

WASHBURNE, Elihu Benjamin
    Whig
    b. Livermore, Me., September 23, 1816
    d. Chicago, Ill., October 22, 1887
    U. S. Representative, 1853-69
    U. S. Secretary of State, 1869

WENTWORTH, John
    Republican
    b. Sandwich, N. H., March 5, 1815
    d. Chicago, Ill., October 16, 1888
    U. S. Representative, 1843-51, 1853-55 (Democrat)
        1865-67 (Republican)

WHARTON, Charles Stuart
    Republican
    b. Aledo, Ill. April 22, 1875
    d. Chicago, Ill., September 4, 1939
    U. S. Representative, 1905-07

WHEAT, William Howard
    Republican
    b. Kahoka, Mo., February 19, 1879
    d. Washington, D. C., January 16, 1944
    U. S. Representative, 1939-44

WHEELER, Hamilton Kinkaid
    Republican
    b. Ballston, N. Y., August 5, 1848
    d. Kankakee, Ill., July 19, 1918
    U. S. Representative, 1893-95

WHEELER, Loren Edgar
    Republican
    b. Havana, Ill., October 7, 1862
    d. Springfield, Ill., January 9, 1932
    U. S. Representative, 1915-23, 1925-27

WHITE, George Elon
    Republican
    b. Millbury, Mass., March 7, 1898
    d. Chicago, Ill., May 17, 1935
    U. S. Representative, 1895-99

WHITING, Richard Henry
    Republican
    b. West Hartford, Conn., January 17, 1826
    d. New York, N. Y., May 24, 1888
    U. S. Representative, 1875-77

WIKE, Scott
    Democrat
    b. Meadville, Pa., April 6, 1834
    d. near Barry, Ill., January 15, 1901
    U. S. Representative, 1875-77, 1889-93

WILLIAMS, James Robert
    Democrat
    b. Carmi, Ill., December 27, 1850
    d. Loma Linda, Calif., November 8, 1923
    U. S. Representative, 1889-95, 1899-1905

WILLIAMS, Thomas Sutler
    Republican
    b. Louisville, Ill., February 14, 1872
    d. Washington, D. C., April 5, 1940
    U. S. Representative, 1915-24

WILLIAMS, William Elza
    Democrat
    b. near Detroit, Mich., May 5, 1857
    d. Pittsfield, Ill., September 13, 1921
    U. S. Representative, 1899-1901, 1913-17

WILSON, William Warfield
    Republican
    b. Ohio, Ill., March 2, 1868
    d. Chicago, Ill., July 22, 1942
    U. S. Representative, 1903-14, 1915-21

WOOD, Benson
    Republican
    b. near Bridgewater, Pa., March 31, 1839
    d. Effingham, Ill., August 27, 1915
    U. S. Representative, 1895-97

WOOD, John
    Republican
    b. Moravia, N. Y., December 20, 1798
    d. June 11, 1880
    Governor of Illinois, 1860-61

WOODMAN, Charles Walhart
    Republican
    b. Aalborg, Denmark, March 11, 1844
    d. Elgin, Ill., March 18, 1898
    U. S. Representative, 1895-97

WOODWORTH, James Hutchinson
    Republican
    b. Greenwich, N. Y., December 4, 1804
    d. Highland Park, Ill., March 26, 1869
    U. S. Representative, 1855-57

WORTHINGTON, Nicholas Ellsworth
    Democrat
    b. Brooke County, Va., March 30, 1836
    d. Peoria, Ill., March 4, 1916
    U. S. Representative, 1883-87

YATES, Richard, Sr.
    Union Republican
    b. Warsaw, Ky., January 18, 1818
    d. St. Louis, Mo., November 27, 1873
    U. S. Representative, 1851-55 (Whig)
    Governor of Illinois, 1861-65
    U. S. Senator, 1865-71 (Union Republican)

YATES, Richard, Jr.
    Republican
    b. Jacksonville, Ill., December 12, 1860
    d. Springfield, Ill., April 11, 1936
    Governor of Illinois, 1901-04
    U. S. Representative, 1919-33

YATES, Sidney Richard
    Democrat
    b. Chicago, Ill., August 27, 1909
    U. S. Representative, 1949-63, 1965-

YOUNG, Richard Montgomery
    Democrat
    b. Fayette County, Ky., February 20, 1798
    d. Washington, D. C., November 28, 1861
    U. S. Senator, 1837-43

YOUNG, Timothy Roberts
    Democrat
    b. Dover, N. H., Nove,ber 19, 1811
    d. Oilfield, near Casey, Ill., May 12, 1898
    U. S. Representative, 1949-51

PROMINENT PERSONALITIES

The following select list of prominent persons of Illinois has been selected to indicate the valuable contributions they have made to American life.

ADDAMS, Jane
    b. September 6, 1860
    d. May 21, 1935
    Opened Hull House, social settlement, with
        Ellen Gates Starr in Chicago, 1889
    Author: Twenty Years at Hull House, 1910
            The Long Road of Women's Memory, 1916
            Peace and Bread in Time of War, 1922
    Shared Nobel Peace Prize with Nicholas Murray
        Butler, 1931

ARMOUR, Philip D.
    b. May 16, 1832
    d. 1901
    Merchant
    Mined in California, 1852-56
    Headed Armour and Company, largest pork-
        packing, dressed meat and provision
        business in the world, from 1875
    Founded Armour Mission and Armour Institute
        of Technology

BACON, Henry
    b. November 28, 1866
    d. February 16, 1924
    Architect
    Designer of Lincoln Memorial
    Member: National Institute of Arts and Letters
            American Academy of Arts and Letters
            National Academy of Design
            Fellow A. I. A.

BENNY, Jack (Benjamin Kubelsky)
    b. Waukegan, Ill., February 14, 1894
    d. December 26, 1974
    Comedian
    began as violinst, 1912
    Featured star in vaudeville, radio, and
        television

BLACK HAWK
    b. Sauk village at Rock River, Ill., 1767
    d. 1838

Sauk Indian Chief
Aided British in War of 1812
Led tribe to resettle their disputed homeland,
    1832 and started Black Hawk War.
Indians defeated and slaughtered at Battle of
    Bad Axe River, Wis., August 2, 1832 -
    Black Hawk imprisoned
Dictated autobiography considered to be classic
    statement of Indian resentment against
    white settlers

BREASTED, James H.
    b. Rockford, Ill.
    Orientalist, Archaeologist and Historian
    Faculty of University of Chicago, 1894-35,
        Professor of Egyptology and Oriental
        History, 1905-35
    Author: A History of Egypt, 1912
            Development of Religion and Thought in
                Ancient Egypt, 1912
            The Dawn of Conscience, 1933

CARPENTER, John Alden
    b. Park Ridge, Ill., February 25, 1876
    d. April 26, 1951
    Composer: Improving Songs with Anxious Child-
        ren (with wife), 1907
            Gitanjali, 1913
            The Birthday of the Infanta - a
                ballet-pantomime, 1919-20
            Skyscrapers - ballet
            Symphony for the 50th Anniversary of
                the Chicago Symphony Orchestra,
                1940

CARTWRIGHT, Peter
    b. Amherst County, Va., September 1, 1785
    d. September 25, 1872
    Ordained deacon, Methodist Church, 1806
    Member of the Illinois legislature
    Ran for Congress against Abraham Lincoln,
        1846, and was defeated

DARROW, Clarence S.
    b. Kinsman, Ohio, April 18, 1857
    d. March 13, 1938
    Attorney
    Defense counsel in several prominent trials:
        Nathan Leopold and Richard Loeb, accused
                of killing Bobbie Franks, 1924
            John Thomas Scopes of Dayton, Tenn.,
                charged with violating a state law
                forbidding the teaching of evolu-

tion in publicly supported schools
and colleges, 1925
Books: Farmington (novel)
Crime, Its Cause and Treatment
The Story of My Life

DEERE, John
b. Rutland, Vt., February 7, 1804
d. May 17, 1886
Manufacturer of steel plows - firm incorporated
as Deere and Company, 1868

DISNEY, Walt (Walter E.)
b. Chicago, Ill., December 5, 1901
d. December 15, 1966
Producer of animated motion picture cartoons
Creator of Oswald, Donald Duck, Mickey Mouse
Successfully produced full-length animated
films:
Snow White and the Seven Dwarfs, 1938
Pinocchio, 1940
Fantasia, 1940
Dumbo, 1941
Bambi, 1942
Peter Pan, 1953
Founder of Disneyland as base of television
productions, 1954
Recipient 39 Awards from the Academy of Motion
Picture Arts and Sciences
4 Emmy Awards

DOS PASSOS, John
b. Chicago, 1896
Author: Manhattan Transfers, 1925
The 42nd Parallel, 1930
Number One, 1943

FARRELL, James T.
b. Chicago, Ill., February 27, 1904
Author: Gas House McGinty, 1933
Studs Lonigan (Trilogy), 1935
No Star Is Lost, 1938
Father and Son, 1940
This Man and This Woman, 1951
The Silence of History, 1963
Invisible Swords, 1971

FIELD, Marshall, b. near Conway, Mass., 1834
d. 1906
Merchant
Became partner in Cooley, Wadsworth and Com-
pany, dry goods firm , 1862
Expanded firm and changed name to the Marshall

Field and Company - became head of firm
to 1906

GARDEN, Mary
b. Scotland, February 20, 1874
d. January 3, 1967
Singer
Début in title role of Charpentier's "Louise"
at Opéra Comique, Paris, April 13, 1900
U. S. début, "Thais," November 25. 1907
Appeared with Chicago Grand Opera Company,
1910-31

GRANT, Ulysses S.
b. Point Pleasant, Ohio, April 27, 1822
d. Mount McGregor, N. Y., July 23, 1885
Appointed Brigadier General, 1861
Captured Vicksburg, July 4, 1863
Promoted to Lieutenant General, 1863, commander of Union Armies under Lincoln
Received Lee's surrender, Appomatox Court
House, April 9, 1865
18th President of the United States, 1869-
77

HEMINGWAY, Ernest
b. Oak Park, Ill., July 21, 1899
d. July 2, 1961
War correspondent, Spanish Civil War, 1937-38;
China, 1941; World War II, 1944-45
Author: In Our Time, 1924
The Sun Also Rises, 1926
Men Without Women, 1927
A Farewell to Arms, 1929
To Have and Have Not, 1937
For Whom the Bell Tolls, 1940
The Old Man and the Sea, 1952
Awarded: Pulitzer Prize in Fiction, 1953
Nobel Prize in Literature, 1954

IVES, Burl
b. Hunt, Ill., June 14, 1909
Singer and actor
Travelled in 46 states as troubadour - collected
and sang American folk songs
Movies: Cat on a Hot Tin Roof
Our Man in Havana
Television: The Bold Ones, 1970-72

LINDSAY, Vachel (Nicholas Vachel)
b. Springfield, Ill., November 10, 1879
d. December 5, 1931
Poet

Works: <u>General William Booth Enters Into Heaven</u>
<u>and Other Poems</u>, 1913
<u>The Congo and Other Poems</u>, 1914
<u>The Chinese Nightingale</u>, 1917
<u>Going-to-the-Sun</u>, 1923

MACLEISH, Archibald
b. Glencoe, Ill., May 7, 1892
Poet and writer
Professor at Harvard, 1949-62
Lecturer at Amherst College, 1963-67
Pulitzer Prize in Poetry, 1932, 1953
Pulitzer Prize in Drama, 1959
Works: <u>The Happy Marriage</u>, 1924
<u>New Found Land</u>, 1930
<u>Land of the Free</u>, 1938
<u>Act Five</u>, 1948
<u>Eleanor Roosevelt Story</u>, 1965
<u>Scratch</u>, 1971

MASTERS, Edgar Lee
b. Garnett, Kansas, August 23, 1869
d. March 5, 1950
Author
Awarded first $5,000 fellowship granted by the
Academy of American Poets
Works: <u>Blood of the Prophets</u>, 1905
<u>Spoon River Anthology</u>, 1915
<u>Mark Twain</u>, 1938
<u>Ilinois Poems</u>, 1941

MCCORMICK, Cyrus H.
b. Walnut Grove, Va., February 15, 1809
d. May 13, 1884
Manufacturer and inventor
Invented and patented hillside plough, 1831;
patented reaping machine, 1834
Erected factory to manufacture farm machinery
in Chicago, 1847
Became owner of Chicago <u>Times</u>, 1860
Pioneer in creating modern business techniques

MCCORMICK, Robert Rutherford
b. Chicago, Ill., July 3, 1880
d. April 1, 1955
President of Sanitary District of Chicago, 1905-
10
Editor and publisher of Chicago <u>Tribune</u>, 1920-55

MOODY, Dwight L.
b. Northfield, Mass., February 5, 1837
d. 1899
Evangelist

Organized North Market Sabbath School, Chicago,
    1858
Founded Northfield Seminary for girls, 1879
Founded Mount Hebron School for boys, 1881
Founded Chicago Bible Institute (now called
    Moody Bible Institute), 1889

MARQUIS, Donald (Don) Robert Perry
    b. Walnut, Ill., July 29, 1878
    d. December 29, 1937
    Staff member, New York Sun, 1912-22
    Staff member, New York Tribune, 1922-25
    Author
    Works: The Old Soak, 1921
            archy and mehitabel, 1927
            Off the Arm, 1930
            archy does his part, 1935

NEWBERRY, Walter Loomis
    b. East Windsor, Conn., September 18, 1804
    d. November 6, 1868
    Adjutant General, Territory of Michigan, 1829-31
    Founder and Director of Merchants Loan and
            Trust Company, beginning 1857
    Acting Mayor of Chicago, 1851
    Half of estate used to found the Newberry
        Library, an independent free public
        library in Chicago

PARRINGTON, Vernon L.
    b. Aurora, Ill., August 3, 1871
    d. June 16, 1929
    Faculty member, Department of English, University
            of Oklahoma, 1877-1908
    Professor of English, University of Washington,
            1908-29
    Author
    Works: Main Currents in American Thought: An In-
            terpretation of American Literature
            from the Beginning to 1920 (3 vols.),
            1927-30

POPE, Nathaniel
    b. Louisville, Ky., January 5, 1784
    d. January 22, 1850
    U. S. District Judge for Illinois, 1819-50

SANDBURG, Carl
    b. Galesburg, Ill., January 6, 1878
    d. July 22, 1967
    Poet and author
    Pulitzer Prize in Poetry, 1950
    Gold Medal for History, American Academy of Arts

and Letters, 1952, 1953
Gold Medal for Poetry, Poetry Society of America
Poetry: <u>Chicago Poems</u>, 1915
         <u>Corn Huskers</u>, 1918
         <u>Good Morning, America</u>, 1928
         <u>The People, Yes</u>, 1936
Biographies: <u>Abraham Lincoln - The Prairie
             Years</u>, 1926
             <u>Steichen The Photographer</u>, 1929

SMITH, Joseph
     b. Sharon, Vt., December 23, 1805
     d. June 27, 1844
     Mormon prophet
     Began to have visions, 1820
     Published <u>The Book of Mormon</u>, 1830
     Founded Church of Jesus Christ of Latter-Day
          Saints, Fayette, N. Y., April 6, 1830
     Moved congregation to Kirtland, Ohio, 1831
     Moved to Missouri, 1838
     Moved to Commerce, Ill. (renamed Nauvoo)
     Killed by mob opposed to polygamy, June 27, 1844

 STRITCH, Samuel Alphonsus
     b. Nashville, Tenn., August 17, 1887
     d. May 27, 1958
     Ordained Roman Catholic priest, 1910
     Appointed Bishop of Toledo, August 1921
     Appointed Archbishop of Milwaukee, April 26,
          1930
     Appointed Archbishop of Chicago, December 27,
          1939
     Appointed Cardinal by Pope Pius XII, December
          1945

SULLIVAN, Louis H.
     b. Boston, Mass., September 3, 1856
     d. April 14, 1924
     Architect
     Regarded as father of modernism in architecture
     Notable buildings: Auditorium Building, Chicago
     Transportation Building, World's Columbian Expo-
          sition, 1893
     Wainwright Building and Union Trust Building,
          St. Louis
     Gage Building and Stock Exchange Building,
          Chicago
     Bayard Building, New York

SWIFT, Gustav Franklin
     b. near Sandwich, Mass., June 24, 1839
     d. 1903
     Made first shipment of dressed beef to East, 1877

Profited by utilizing meat by-products to make
     oleo-margarine, soap, glue, and other
     items.
Incorporated business as Swift and Company,
     1885

TONTI, Henri de (Henry de Tonty)
     b. Gaeta, Italy, 1650
     d. 1704
     Explorer with La Salle, built Fort Crevecoeur
          on Lake Peoria, 1679-80
     Built Fort St. Louis on the Illinois River,
          1681-82
     Brought settlers from Canada to Illinois
     Joined Le Moyne's settlement near mouth of
          Mississippi River, 1700

TURNER, Jonathan Baldwin
     b. Templeton, Mass., December 7, 1805
     d. January 10, 1899
     Professor of Rhetoric and Belles-Lettres,
          Illinois College, Jacksonville
     Organizer of the Illinois Teachers Associa-
          tion, 1836
     First president of the Illinois Natural
          History Society
     One of founders of Industrial School which
          became the University of Illinois

WILLIAMS, Daniel Hale
     b. Hollidaysburg, Pa., January 18, 1858
     d. August 4, 1931
     Physician
     Surgeon-in-chief, Freedmen's Hospital,
          Washington, D. C., 1893-98
     Member of staff, St. Luke's Hospital, Chicago
     Member Illinois State Board of Health, 1889,
          reappointed, 1891
     Fellow American College of Surgeons
     Professor of Clinical Surgery, Meharry Medical
          College, Tennessee

WRIGHT, Frank Lloyd
     b. Richland Center, Wis., June 8, 1869
     d. April 9, 1959
     Work in America classified as "the new school
          of the Middle West"
     Europeans viewed his work as "the American
          expression in architecture"
     Granted many honors and awards
     Wrote many books
     Editor of magazine: Teliesin

FIRST STATE CONSTITUTION

STATEHOOD PERIOD

New states were rapidly being added to the Union at this time – Indiana in 1816, Mississippi in 1817, with Alabama and Missouri organizing with the same objective in view. There was concern lest the Illinois country be left as a territorial island between new states to east and west, each establishing its advantageous foothold in Congress. Although, as in most territories, there was some opposition to statehood from those who had found positions of advantage in the existing situation, most of the factional rivalries of the earlier years had been dispelled, under the leadership of Governor Ninian Edwards and the editor of the territory's only newspaper, Daniel Pope Cook. The statehood convention, accordingly, met the approval of a substantial majority of these men's followers when it met at Kaskaskia on August 1, 1818.

Constitution of 1818

Source: 1 Poore, *Charters and Constitutions*, 439-49

The people of the Illinois Territory, having the right of admission into the General Government as a member of the Union, consistent with the Constitution of the United States, the ordinance of Congress of 1787, and the law of Congress approved April 18, 1818, entitled "An act to enable the people of the Illinois Territory to form a constitution and State government, and for the admission of such State into the Union, on an equal footing with the original States, and for other purposes," in order to establish justice, promote the welfare, and secure the blessings of liberty to themselves and their posterity, do, by their representatives in convention, ordain and establish the following constitution or form of government; and do mutually agree with each other to form themselves into a free and independent State, by the name of the State of Illinois. And they do hereby ratify the boundaries assigned to such State by the act of Congress aforesaid, which are as follows, to wit: Beginning at the mouth of the Wabash River; thence up the same and with the line of Indiana to the northwest corner of said State; thence east with the line of the same State to the middle of Lake Michigan; thence north, along the middle of said lake, to north latitude forty-two degrees and thirty minutes; thence west to the middle of the Mississippi River; and thence down along the middle of that river to its confluence with the Ohio River; and thence up the latter river, along its northwestern shore, to the beginning.

ARTICLE I.

SECTION 1. The powers of the government of the State of Illinois shall be divided into three distinct departments, and each of them be confided to a separate body of magistracy, to wit: Those which are legislative, to one; those which are executive, to another; and those which are judiciary, to another.

SEC. 2. No person or collection of persons being one of those departments shall exercise any power properly belonging to either of the others, except as hereinafter expressly directed or permitted.

ARTICLE II.

SECTION 1. The legislative authority of this State shall be vested in a general assembly, which shall consist in a senate and house of representatives, both to be elected by the people.

SEC. 2. The first election for senators and representatives shall commence on the third Thursday of September next, and continue for that and the two succeeding days; and the next election shall be held on the first Monday in August, 1820; and forever after elections shall be held once in two years, on the first Monday of August, in each and every county, at such places therein as may be provided by law.

SEC. 3. No person shall be a representative who shall not have attained the age of twenty-one years; who shall not be a citizen of the United States, and an inhabitant of this State; who shall not have resided within the limits of the county or district in which he shall be chosen twelve months next preceding his election, if such county or district shall have been so long erected; but if not, then within the limits of the county or counties, district or districts, out of which the same shall have been taken, unless he shall have been absent on the public business of the United States or of this State, and who, moreover, shall not have paid a State or county tax.

SEC. 4. The senators, at their first session herein provided for, shall be divided by lot from their respective counties or districts, as near as can be, into two classes. The seats of the senators of the first class shall be vacated at the expiration of the second year, and those of the second class at the expiration of the fourth year, so that one-half thereof, as near as possible, may be biennially chosen forever thereafter.

SEC. 5. The number of senators and representatives shall, at the first session of the general assembly holden after the returns herein provided for are made, be fixed by the general assembly, and apportioned among the several counties or districts to be established by law, according to the number of white inhabitants. The number of representatives shall not be less than twenty-six, nor more than thirty-six, until the number of inhabitants within this State shall amount to one hundred thousand; and the number of senators shall never be less than one-third nor more than one-half of the number of representatives.

SEC. 6. No person shall be a senator who has not arrived at the age of twenty-five years, who shall not be a citizen of the United States, and who shall not have resided one year in the county or district in which he shall be chosen immediately preceding his election, if such county or district shall have been so long erected; but if not, then within the limits of the county or counties, district or districts, out of which the same shall have been taken, unless he shall have been absent on the public business of the United States or of this State, and shall not, moreover, have paid a State or county tax.

SEC. 7. The senate and house of representatives, when assembled, shall each choose a speaker and other officers, (the speaker of the senate excepted.) Each house shall judge of the qualifications and elections of its members, and sit upon its own adjournments. Two-thirds of each house shall constitute a quorum, but a smaller number may adjourn from day to day, and compel the attendance of absent members.

SEC. 8. Each house shall keep a journal of its proceedings and publish them. The yeas and nays of the members on any question shall, at the desire of any two of them, be entered on the journals.

SEC. 9. Any two members of either house shall have liberty to dissent and protest against any act or resolution which they may think injurious to the public, or to any individual, and have the reasons of their dissent entered on the journals.

SEC. 10. Each house may determine the rules of its proceedings, punish its members for disorderly behavior, and, with the concurrence of two-thirds, expel a member, but not a second time for the same cause.

SEC. 11. When vacancies happen in either house, the governor, or the person exercising the powers of governor, shall issue writs of election to fill such vacancies.

SEC. 12. Senators and representatives shall in all cases, except treason, felony, or breach of the peace, be privileged from arrest during the session of the general assembly, and in going to or returning from the same; and for any speech or debate in either house they shall not be questioned in any other place.

SEC. 13. Each house may punish, by imprisonment during its session, any person not a member who shall be guilty of disrespect to the house, by any disorderly or contemptuous behavior in their presence; provided such imprisonment shall not at any one time exceed twenty-four hours.

SEC. 14. The doors of each house and of committees of the whole shall be kept open, except in such cases as in the opinion of the house require secrecy. Neither house shall, without the consent of the other, adjourn for more than two days, nor to any other place than that in which the two houses shall be sitting.

SEC. 15. Bills may originate in either house, but may be altered, amended, or rejected by the other.

SEC. 16. Every bill shall be read on three different days in each house, unless, in case of urgency, three-fourths of the house where such bill is so depending shall deem it expedient to dispense with this rule; and every bill having passed both houses shall be signed by the speakers of the respective houses.

SEC. 17. The style of the laws of this State shall be, "*Be it enacted by the people of the State of Illinois, represented in the general assembly.*"

SEC. 18. The general assembly of this State shall not allow the following officers of government greater or smaller annual salaries than as follows, until the year 1824: The governor, $1,000; and the secretary of state, $600.

SEC. 19. No senator or representative shall, during the time for which he shall have been elected, be appointed to any civil office under this State, which shall have been created, or the emoluments of which shall have been increased, during such time.

SEC. 20. No money shall be drawn from the treasury but in consequence of appropriations made by law.

SEC. 21. An accurate statement of the receipts and expenditures of the public money shall be attached to and published with the laws, at the rising of each session of the general assembly.

SEC. 22. The house of representatives shall have the sole power of impeaching, but a majority of all the members present must concur in an impeachment. All impeachments shall be tried by the senate, and when sitting for that purpose the senators shall be upon oath or affirmation to do justice according to law and evidence. No person shall be convicted without the concurrence of two-thirds of all the senators present.

SEC. 23. The governor, and all other civil officers under this State, shall be liable to impeachment for any misdemeanor in office; but judgment in such cases shall not extend further than to removal from office, and disqualification to hold any office of honor, profit, or trust under this State. The party, whether convicted or acquitted, shall nevertheless be liable to indictment, trial, judgment, and punishment according to law.

SEC. 24. The first session of the general assembly shall commence on the first Monday of October next, and forever after the general assembly shall meet on the first Monday in December next ensuing the election of the members thereof, and at no other period, unless as provided by this constitution.

SEC. 25. No judge of any court of law or equity, secretary of state, attorney-general, attorney for the State, register, clerk of any court of record, sheriff, or collector, member of either house of Congress, or person holding any lucrative office under the United States or this State, (provided that appointments in the militia, postmasters, or justices of the peace shall not be considered lucrative offices,) shall have a seat in the general assembly; nor shall any person holding any office of honor or profit under the Government of the United States hold any office of honor or profit under the authority of this State.

SEC. 26. Every person who shall be chosen or appointed to any office of trust or profit shall, before entering upon the duties thereof, take an oath to support the Constitution of the United States and of this State, and also an oath of office.

[1] SEC. 27. In all elections, all white male inhabitants above the age of twenty-one years, having resided in the State six months next preceding the election, shall enjoy the right of an elector; but no person shall be entitled to vote except in the county or district in which he shall actually reside at the time of the election.

SEC. 28. All votes shall be given *viva voce* until altered by the general assembly.

SEC. 29. Electors shall, in all cases, except treason, felony, or breach of the peace, be privileged from arrest during their attendance at elections, and in going to and returning from the same.

SEC. 30. The general assembly shall have full power to exclude from the privilege of electing or being elected any person convicted of bribery, perjury, or any other infamous crime.

SEC. 31. In the year 1820, and every fifth year thereafter, an enumeration of all the white inhabitants of the State shall be made in such manner as shall be directed by law.

SEC. 32. All bills for raising a revenue shall originate in the house of representatives, subject, however, to amendment or rejection as in other cases.

ARTICLE III.

[2] SECTION 1. The executive power of the State shall be vested in a governor.

SEC. 2. The first election of governor shall commence on the third Thursday of September next, and continue for that and the two succeeding days; and the next election shall be held on the first Monday of August, in the year of our Lord 1822. And forever after, elections for governor shall be held once in four years, on the first Monday in August. The governor shall be chosen by the electors of the members of the general assembly, at the same places and in the same manner that they shall respectively vote for members thereof. The returns for every election of governor shall be sealed up and transmitted to the seat of government by the returning officers, directed to the speaker of the house of representatives, who shall open and publish them in the presence of a majority of the members of each house of the general assembly. The person having the highest number of votes shall be governor; but if two or more be equal and highest in votes, then one of them shall be chosen governor by joint ballot of both houses of the general assembly. Contested elections shall be determined by both houses of the general assembly in such manner as shall be prescribed by law.

SEC. 3. The first governor shall hold his office until the first Monday of December, in the year of our Lord 1822, and until another governor shall be elected and qualified to office; and forever after the governor shall hold his office for the term of four years and until another governor shall be elected and qualified; but he shall not be eligible for more than four years in any term of eight years. He shall be at least thirty years of age, and have been a citizen of the United States thirty years; two years of which next preceding his election he shall have resided within the limits of this State.

SEC. 4. He shall, from time to time, give the general assembly information of the state of the government, and recommend to their consideration such measures as he shall deem expedient.

SEC. 5. He shall have power to grant reprieves and pardons after conviction, except in cases of impeachment.

SEC. 6. The governor shall, at stated times, receive a salary for his services, which shall neither be increased nor diminished during the term for which he shall have been elected.

SEC. 7. He may require information in writing from the officers in the executive department, upon any subject relating to the duties of their respective offices, and shall take care that the laws be faithfully executed.

SEC. 8. When any officer, the right of whose appointment is, by this constitution, vested in the general assembly, or in the governor and senate, shall, during the recess, die, or his office by any means become vacant, the governor shall have power to fill such vacancy, by granting a commission, which shall expire at the end of the next session of the general assembly.

SEC. 9. He may, on extraordinary occasions, convene the general assembly by proclamation, and shall state to them, when assembled, the purpose for which they shall have been convened.

SEC. 10. He shall be commander-in-chief of the army and navy of this State, and of the militia, except when they shall be called into the service of the United States.

SEC. 11. There shall be elected in each and every county in the said State, by those who are qualified to vote for members of the general assembly, and at the same time and places where the election for such members shall be held, one sheriff and one coroner, whose election shall be subject to such rules and regulations as shall be prescribed by law. The said sheriffs and coroners respectively, when elected, shall continue in office two years, be subject to removal and disqualification, and such other rules and regulations as may be from time to time prescribed by law.

SEC. 12. In case of disagreement between two houses with respect to the time of adjournment, the governor shall have power to adjourn the general assembly to such time as he thinks proper, provided it be not a period beyond the next constitutional meeting of the same.

SEC. 13. A lieutenant-governor shall be chosen at every election for governor in the same manner, continue in office for the same time, and possess the same qualifications. In voting for governor and lieutenant-governor, the electors shall distinguish whom they vote for as governor and whom as lieutenant-governor.

SEC. 14. He shall, by virtue of his office, be speaker of the senate, have a right, when in committee of the whole, to debate and vote on all subjects, and whenever the senate are equally divided, to give the casting vote.

SEC. 15. Whenever the government shall be administered by the lieutenant-governor, or he shall be unable to attend as speaker of the senate, the senators shall elect one of their own members as speaker for that occasion; and if, during the vacancy of the office of governor, the lieutenant-governor shall be impeached, removed from office, ruse to qualify, or resign, or die, or be absent from the State, the speaker of the senate shall in like manner administer the government.

SEC. 16. The lieutenant-governor, while he acts as speaker of the senate, shall receive for his services the same compensation which shall, for the same period, be allowed to the speaker of the house of representatives and no more; and during the time he administers the government as governor, he shall receive the same compensation which the governor would have received had he been employed in the duties of his office.

SEC. 17. If the lieutenant-governor shall be called upon to administer the government, and shall, while in such administration, resign, die, or be absent from the State during the recess of the general assembly, it shall be the duty of the secretary for the time being to convene the senate for the purpose of choosing a speaker.

SEC. 18. In case of an impeachment of the governor, his removal from office, death, refusal to qualify, resignation or absence from the State, the lieutenant-governor shall exercise all the power and authority appertaining to the office of governor, until the time pointed out by this constitution for the election of governor shall arrive, unless the general assembly shall provide by law for the election of a governor to fill such vacancy.

SEC. 19. The governor for the time being, and the judges of the supreme court or a major part of them, together with the governor, shall be, and are hereby, constituted a council to revise all bills about to be passed into laws by the general assembly; and for that purpose shall assemble themselves from time to time when the general assembly shall be convened, for which nevertheless they shall not receive any salary or consideration under any pretence whatever; and all bills which have passed the senate and house of representatives shall, before they become laws, be presented to the said council for their revisal and consideration; and if, upon such revisal and consideration, it should appear improper to the said council or a majority of them, that the bill should become a law of this State, they shall return the same, together with their objections thereto, in writing, to the senate or house of representatives, (in whichsoever the same shall have originated,) who shall enter the objections set down by the council at large in their minutes, and proceed to reconsider the said bill. But if, after such reconsideration, the said senate or house of representatives shall, notwithstanding the said objections, agree to pass the same by a majority of the whole number of members elected, it shall, together with the said objections, be sent to the other branch of the general assembly, where it shall also be reconsidered, and if approved by a majority of all the members elected, it shall become a law. If any bill shall not be returned within ten days after it shall have been presented, the same shall be a law, unless the general assembly shall by their adjournment, render a return of the said bill in ten days impracticable; in which case the said bill shall be returned on the first day of the meeting of the general assembly, after the expiration of the said ten days, or be a law.

SEC. 20. The governor shall nominate, and by and with the advice and consent of the senate appoint, a secretary of state, who shall keep a fair register of the official acts of the governor, and, when required, shall lay the same, and all papers, minutes, and vouchers relative thereto, before either branch of the general assembly, and shall perform such other duties as shall be assigned him by law.

SEC. 21. The State treasurer and public printer or printers for the State shall be appointed biennially by the joint vote of both branches of the general assembly: *Provided*, That during the recess of the same the governor shall have power to fill such vacancies as may happen in either of said offices.

SEC. 22. The governor shall nominate, and by and with the advice and consent of the senate appoint, all officers whose offices are established by this constitution, or shall be established by law, and whose appointments are not herein otherwise provided for: *Provided, however,* That inspectors, collectors, and their deputies, surveyors of the highways, constables, jailers, and such inferior officers whose jurisdiction may be confined within the limits of the county, shall be appointed in such manner as the general assembly shall prescribe.

ARTICLE IV.

SECTION 1. The judicial power of this State shall be vested in one supreme court, and such inferior courts as the general assembly shall, from time to time, ordain and establish.

SEC. 2. The supreme court shall be holden at the seat of government, and shall have an appellate jurisdiction only, except in cases relating to the revenue, in cases of *mandamus,* and in such cases of impeachment as may be required to be tried before it.

SEC. 3. The supreme court shall consist in a chief-justice and three associates, any two of whom shall form a quorum. The number of justices may, however, be increased by the general assembly after the year 1824.

SEC. 4. The justices of the supreme court and the judges of the inferior courts shall be appointed by joint ballot of both branches of the general assembly, and commissioned by the governor, and shall hold their offices during good behavior until the end of the first session of the general assembly, which shall be begun and held after the 1st day of January, in the year of our Lord 1824, at which time their commissions shall expire; and until the expiration of which time the said justices, respectively, shall hold circuit courts in the several counties, in such manner, and at such times, and shall have and exercise such jurisdiction as the general assembly shall by law prescribe. But ever after the aforesaid period the justices of the supreme court shall be commissioned during good behavior, and the justices thereof shall not hold circuit courts unless required by law.

SEC. 5. The judges of the inferior courts shall hold their offices during good behavior, but for any reasonable cause, which shall not be sufficient ground for impeachment, both the judges of the supreme and inferior courts shall be removed from office on the address of two-thirds of each branch of the general assembly: *Provided always*, That no member of either house of the general assembly, nor any person connected with a member by consanguinity or affinity, shall be appointed to fill the vacancy occasioned by such removal. The said justices of the supreme court, during their temporary appointment, shall receive an annual salary of one thousand dollars, payable quarter-yearly out of the public treasury. The judges of the inferior courts, and the justices of the supreme court who may be appointed after the end of the first session of the general assembly which shall be begun and held after the first day of January, in the year of our Lord 1824, shall have adequate and competent salaries, which shall not be diminished during their continuance in office.

SEC. 6. The supreme court, or a majority of the justices thereof, the circuit courts, or the justices thereof, shall, respectively, appoint their own clerks.

SEC. 7. All process, writs, and other proceedings shall run in the name of "The people of the State of Illinois." All prosecutions shall be carried on "In the name and by the authority of the people of the State of Illinois," and conclude "Against the peace and dignity of the same."

SEC. 8. A competent number of justices of the peace shall be appointed in each county, in such manner as the general assembly may direct, whose time of service, power, and duties shall be regulated and defined by law. And justices of the peace, when so appointed, shall be commissioned by the governor.

ARTICLE V.

SECTION 1. The militia of the State of Illinois shall consist of all free, male, able-bodied persons, (negroes, mulattoes, and Indians excepted,) resident in the State, between the age of eighteen and forty-five years, (except such persons as now are, or hereafter may be, exempted by the law of the United States or of this State,) and shall be armed, equipped, and trained as the general assembly may provide by law.

SEC. 2. No person or persons conscientiously scrupulous of bearing arms shall be compelled to do militia duty in time of peace: *Provided*, Such person or persons shall pay an equivalent for such exemptions.

SEC. 3. Company, battalion, and regimental officers, staff officers excepted, shall be elected by the persons composing their several companies, battalions, and regiments.

SEC. 4. Brigadier and major generals shall be elected by the officers of their brigades and divisions respectively.

SEC. 5. All militia officers shall be commissioned by the governor, and may hold their commissions during good behavior, or until they arrive at the age of sixty years.

SEC. 6. The militia shall in all cases, except treason, felony, or breach of the peace, be privileged from arrest during their attendance at musters and elections of officers, and in going to and returning from the same.

ARTICLE VI.

SECTION 1. Neither slavery nor involuntary servitude shall hereafter be introduced into this State, otherwise than for the punishment of crimes, whereof the party shall have been duly convicted; nor shall any male person, arrived at the age of twenty-one years, nor female person arrived at the age of eighteen years, be held to serve any person as a servant, under any indenture hereafter made, unless such person shall enter into such indenture while in a state of perfect freedom, and on condition of a *bona-fide* consideration received or to be received for their service. Nor shall any indenture of any negro or mulatto, hereafter made and executed out of this State, or if made in this State, where the term of service exceeds one year, be of the least validity, except those given in cases of apprenticeship.

SEC. 2. No person bound to labor in any other State shall be hired to labor in this State, except within the tract reserved for the salt-works near Shawneetown; nor even at that place for a longer period than one year at any one time; nor shall it be allowed there after the year 1825. Any violation of this article shall effect the emancipation of such person from his obligation to service.

SEC. 3. Each and every person who has been bound to service by contract or indenture in virtue of the laws of Illinois Territory heretofore existing, and in conformity to the provisions of the same, without fraud or collusion, shall be held to a specific performance of their contracts or indentures; and such negroes and mulattoes as have been registered in conformity with the aforesaid laws shall serve out the time appointed by said laws: *Provided, however,* That the children hereafter born of such person, negroes, or mulattoes, shall become free, the males at the age of twenty-one years, the females at the age of eighteen years. Each and every child born of indentured parents shall be entered with the clerk of the county in which they reside, by their owners, within six months after the birth of said child.

ARTICLE VII.

SECTION 1. Whenever two-thirds of the general assembly shall think it necessary to alter or amend this constitution, they shall recommend to the electors, at the next election of members to the general assembly, to vote for or against a convention; and if it shall appear that a majority of all the citizens of the State, voting for representatives, have voted for a convention, the general assembly shall, at their next session, call a convention, to consist of as many members as there may be in the general assembly, to be chosen in the same manner, at the same place, and by the same electors that choose the general assembly; and which convention shall meet within three months after said election, for the purpose of revising, altering, or amending this constitution.

ARTICLE VIII.

That the general, great, and essential principles of liberty and free government may be recognized and unalterably established, we declare:

SECTION 1. That all men are born equally free and independent, and have certain inherent and indefeasible rights; among which are those of enjoying and defending life and liberty, and of acquiring, possessing, and protecting property and reputation, and of pursuing their own happiness.

SEC. 2. That all power is inherent in the people, and all free governments are founded on their authority, and instituted for their peace, safety, and happiness.

SEC. 3. That all men have a natural and indefeasible right to worship Almighty God according to the dictates of their own consciences; that no man can of right be compelled to attend, erect, or support any place of worship, or to maintain any ministry against his consent; that no human authority can, in any case whatever, control or interfere with the rights of conscience; and that no preference shall ever be given by law to any religious establishments or modes of worship.

SEC. 4. That no religious test shall ever be required as a qualification to any office or public trust under this State.

SEC. 5. That elections shall be free and equal.

SEC. 6. That the right of the trial by jury shall remain inviolate.

SEC. 7. That the people shall be secure in their persons, houses, papers, and possessions from unreasonable searches and seizures; and that general warrants, whereby an officer may be commanded to search suspected places without evidence of the fact committed, or to seize any person or persons not named, whose offences are not particularly described and supported by evidence, are dangerous to liberty, and ought not to be granted.

SEC. 8. That no freeman shall be imprisoned or disseized of his freehold, liberties, or privileges, or outlawed or exiled, or in any manner deprived of his life, liberty, or property, but by the judgment of his peers or the law of the land. And all lands which have been granted as a common to the inhabitants of any town, hamlet, village, or corporation, by any person, body politic or corporate, or by any government having power to make such grant, shall forever remain common to the inhabitants of such town, hamlet, village, or corporation; and the said commons shall not be leased, sold, or divided under any pretence whatever: *Provided, however,* That nothing in this section shall be so construed as to affect the commons of Cahokia or Prairie du Pont: *Provided also*, That the general assembly shall have power and authority to grant the same privileges to the inhabitants of the said villages of Cahokia and Prairie du Pont as are hereby granted to the inhabitants of other towns, hamlets, and villages.

SEC. 9. That in all criminal prosecutions, the accused hath a right to be heard by himself and counsel; to demand the nature and cause of the accusation against him; to meet the witnesses face to face; to have compulsory process to compel the attendance of witnesses in his favor; and in prosecutions by indictment or information, a speedy public trial by an impartial jury of the vicinage; and that he shall not be compelled to give evidence against himself.

SEC. 10. That no person shall, for any indictable offence, be proceeded against criminally by information, except in cases arising in the land or naval forces, or the militia when in actual service, in time of war, or public danger, by leave of the courts, for oppression or misdemeanor in office.

SEC. 11. No person shall, for the same offence, be twice put in jeopardy of his life or limb; nor shall any man's property be taken or applied to public use, without the consent of his representatives in the general assembly, nor without just compensation being made to him.

SEC. 12. Every person within this State ought to find a certain remedy in the laws for all injuries or wrongs which he may receive in his person, property, or character; he ought to obtain right and justice freely, and without being obliged to purchase it, completely and without denial, promptly and without delay, conformably to the laws.

SEC. 13. That all persons shall be bailable by sufficient sureties, unless for capital offences, where the proof is evident or the presumption great; and the privilege of the writ of *habeas corpus* shall not be suspended, unless when, in case of rebellion or invasion, the public safety may require it.

SEC. 14. All penalties shall be proportioned to the nature of the offence, the true design of all punishment being to reform, not to exterminate, mankind.

SEC. 15. No person shall be imprisoned for debt, unless upon refusal to deliver up his estate for the benefit of his creditors, in such manner as shall be prescribed by law, or in cases where there is strong presumption of fraud.

SEC. 16. No *ex post facto* law, nor any law impairing the validity of contracts, shall ever be made; and no conviction shall work corruption of blood or forfeiture of estate.

SEC. 17. That no person shall be liable to be transported out of this State for any offence committed within the same.

SEC. 18. That a frequent recurrence to the fundamental principles of civil government is absolutely necessary to preserve the blessings of liberty.

SEC. 19. That the people have a right to assemble together in a peaceable manner to consult for their common good, to instruct their representatives, and to apply to the general assembly for redress of grievances.

SEC. 20. That the mode of levying a tax shall be by valuation, so that every person shall pay a tax in proportion to the value of the property he or she has in his or her possession.

SEC. 21. That there shall be no other banks or moneyed institutions in this State but those already provided by law, except a State bank and its branches, which may be established and regulated by the general assembly of the State as they may think proper.

SEC. 22. The printing-presses shall be free to every person who undertakes to examine the proceedings of the general assembly or of any branch of government; and no law shall ever be made to restrain the right thereof. The free communication of thoughts and opinions is one of the invaluable rights of man, and every citizen may freely speak, write, and print on any subject, being responsible for the abuse of that liberty.

SEC. 23. In prosecutions for the publication of papers investigating the official conduct of officers, or of men acting in a public capacity, or where the matter published is proper for public information, the truth thereof may be given in evidence. And in all indictments for libels the jury shall have the right of determining both the law and the fact, under the direction of the court, as in other cases.

SCHEDULE.

SECTION 1. That no inconveniences may arise from the change of a territorial to a permanent State government, it is declared by the convention that all rights, suits, actions, prosecutions, claims, and contracts, both as it respects individuals and bodies-corporate, shall continue as if no change had taken place in this government in virtue of the laws now in force.

SEC. 2. All fines, penalties, and forfeitures due and owing to the Territory of Illinois shall inure to the use of the State. All bonds executed to the governor, or to any other officer in his official capacity in the Territory, shall pass over to the governor or to the officers of the State, and their successors in office, for the use of the State, by him or by them to be respectively assigned over to the use of those concerned, as the case may be.

SEC. 3. No sheriff or collector of public moneys shall be eligible to any office in this State, until they have paid over, according to law, all moneys which they may have collected by virtue of their respective offices.

SEC. 4. There shall be elected in each county three county commissioners for the purpose of transacting all county business, whose time of service, power, and duties shall be regulated and defined by law.

SEC. 5. The governor, secretary, and judges, and all other officers under the territorial government, shall continue in the exercise of the duties of their respective departments until the said officers are superseded under the authority of this constitution.

SEC. 6. The governor of this State shall make use of his private seal until a State seal shall be provided.

SEC. 7. The oaths of office herein directed to be taken may be administered by any justice of the peace until the general assembly shall otherwise direct.

SEC. 8. [Apportionment of senators and representatives.*]

SEC. 9. The president of the convention shall issue writs of election, directed to the several sheriffs of the several counties, or in case of the absence or disability of any sheriff, then to the deputy sheriff, and in case of the absence or disability of the deputy sheriff, then such writ to be directed to the coroner, requiring them to cause an election to be held for governor, lieutenant-governor, Representative to the present Congress of the United States, and members to the general assembly, and sheriffs and coroners in the respective counties; such election to commence on the third Thursday of September next, and to continue for that and the two succeeding days; and which election shall be conducted in the manner prescribed by the existing election laws of the Illinois Territory; and the said governor, lieutenant-governor, members of the general assembly, sheriffs, and coroners, then duly elected, shall continue to exercise the duties of their respective offices for the time prescribed by this constitution, and until their successor or successors are qualified, and no longer.

SEC. 10. An auditor of public accounts, an attorney-general, and such other officers for the State as may be necessary, may be appointed by the general assembly, whose duties may be regulated by law.

SEC. 11. It shall be the duty of the general assembly to enact such laws as may be necessary and proper to prevent the practice of duelling.

SEC. 12. All white male inhabitants above the age of twenty-one years, who shall be actual residents of this State at the signing of this constitution shall have a right to vote at the election to be held on the third Thursday and the two following days of September next.

SEC. 13. The seat of government for the State shall be at Kaskaskia until the general assembly shall otherwise provide. The general assembly, at their first session holden under the authority of this constitution, shall petition the Congress of the United States to grant to this State a quantity of land, to consist of not more than four, nor less than one section, or to give to this State the right of pre-emption in the purchase of the said quantity of land; the said land to be situate on the Kaskaskia River, and, as near as may be, east of the third principal meridian on said river. Should the prayer of such petition be granted, the general assembly, at their next ses-

sion thereafter, shall provide for the appointment of five commissioners to make the
selection of said land so granted; and shall further provide for laying out a town upon
the land so selected; which town, so laid out, shall be the seat of government of this
State for the term of twenty years. Should, however, the prayer of said petition not
be granted, the general assembly shall have power to make such provisions for a permanent seat of government as may be necessary, and shall fix the same where they
may think best.

SEC. 14. Any person of thirty years of age who is a citizen of the United States and
has resided within the limits of this State two years next preceding his election, shall
be eligible to the office of lieutenant-governor; anything in the thirteenth section of
the third article of this constitution contained to the contrary notwithstanding.

SELECTED DOCUMENTS

The letters selected for this section have been
chosen to illustrate the views of a traveller in Illinois in 1837. Documents relating specifically to
the constitutional development of Illinois will be found
in volume three of <u>Sources and Documents of United States
Constitutions</u>, a companion reference collection to the
Columbia University volumes previously cited.

CHICAGO AS A GROWING VILLAGE

By Patrick Shirreff

SHIRREFF was a Scotch farmer who, in 1833, visited this country for the purpose of studying the adaptability of its various sections to agricultural emigration. His written reports deal primarily with this subject, but comment generally on the country and its inhabitants.

Chicago, which is an Indian word meaning wild onion—a plant which formerly flourished in that vicinity—was laid out as a town in 1830, and was incorporated in 1833. Its first settler was Jean Baptiste Point de Saible, a mulatto refugee who came from Haiti about 1779, and whose cabin-store was acquired in 1804 by John Kinzie, the first white man of American birth to make his home there.

At the time of which this article tells (1833), the Indians sold a large tract of land in the vicinity, agreeing to move across the Mississippi. This they did two years later; and the Fort Dearborn mentioned, being no longer necessary, was abandoned in 1837 and later demolished.

CHICAGO is situated on Lake Michigan, at the confluence of the Chicago River, a small stream, affording the advantages of a canal to the inhabitants for a limited distance. At the mouth of the river is Fort Dearborn, garrisoned by a few soldiers, and one of the places which has been long held to keep the Indian tribes in awe. The entrance from the lake to the river is much obstructed by sand banks, and an attempt is making to improve the navigation.

Chicago consists of about 150 wood houses, placed irregularly on both sides of the river, over which there is a bridge. This is already a place of considerable trade, supplying salt, tea, coffee, sugar and clothing to a large tract

of country to the south and west; and when connected with the navigable point of the river Illinois,
by a canal or railway, cannot fail of rising to importance. Almost every person I met regarded Chicago
as the germ of an immense city, and speculators have
already bought up, at high prices, all the building
ground in the neighborhood. Chicago will, in all
probability, attain considerable size, but its situation is not so favorable to growth as many other places
in the Union. The country south and west of Chicago has a channel of trade to the south by New Orleans; and the navigation from Buffalo by Lake Huron
is of such length, that perhaps the produce of the
country to the south of Chicago will find an outlet
to Lake Erie by the waters of the rivers Wabash and
Mamee. A canal has been in progress for three years,
connecting the Wabash and Mamee, which flows into
the west end of Lake Erie; and there can be little difficulty in connecting the Wabash with the Illinois,
which, if effected, will materially check the rise of
Chicago.

At the time of visiting Chicago, there was a treaty
in progress with the Pottowatamy Indians, and it was
supposed nearly 8000 Indians, of all ages, belonging
to different tribes, were assembled on the occasion,
a treaty being considered a kind of general merry-
making, which lasts several weeks; and animal food,
on the present occasion, was served out by the States
government. The forests and prairies in the neighborhood were studded with the tents of the Indians,

and numerous herds of horses were browsing in all directions.

Some of the tribes could be distinguished by their peculiarities. The Sauks and Foxes have their heads shaven, with exception of a small tuft of hair on the crown. Their garments seemed to vary according to their circumstances, and not to their tribes. The dress of the squaws was generally blue cloth, and sometimes printed cotton, with ornaments in the ears, and occasionally also in the nose. The men generally wore white blankets, with a piece of blue cloth round their loins; and the poorest of them had no other covering, their arms, legs and feet being exposed in nakedness. A few of them had cotton trousers, and jackets of rich patterns, loosely flowing, secured with a sash; boots, and handkerchiefs or bands of cotton, with feathers in the head-dress, their appearance reminding me of the costume of some Asiatic nations. The men are generally without beards, but in one or two instances I saw tufts of hair on the chin, which seemed to be kept with care, and this was conspicuously so among the well-dressed portion. The countenances of both sexes were frequently bedaubed with paint of different kinds, including red, blue and white.

In the forenoon of my arrival, a council had been held, without transacting business, and a race took place in the afternoon. The spectators were Indians, with exception of a few travelers, and their small number showed the affair excited little interest. The riders had a piece of blue cloth round their loins, and in other respects were perfectly naked, having the

whole of their bodies painted of different hues. The
race horses had not undergone a course of training.
They were of ordinary breed, and, according to British
taste at least, small, coarse and ill-formed.

Intoxication prevailed to a great extent among both
sexes. When under the influence of liquor, they did
not seem unusually loquacious, and their chief delight
consisted in venting low shouts, resembling something
between the mewing of a cat and the barking of a dog.
I observed a powerful Indian, stupefied with spirits,
attempting to gain admittance to a shop, vociferating
in a noisy manner; as soon as he reached the highest
step, a white game gave him a push, and he fell with
violence on his back in a pool of mud. He repeated
his attempt five or six times in my sight, and was
uniformly thrown back in the same manner. Male
and female Indians were looking on and enjoying the
sufferings of their countryman. The inhuman wretch
who thus tortured the poor Indian, was the vender of
the poison which had deprived him of his senses.

Besides the assemblage of Indians, there seemed to
be a general fair at Chicago. Large wagons drawn
by six or eight oxen, and heavily laden with merchan-
dise, were arriving from, and departing to, distant
parts of the country. There was also a kind of horse-
market, and I had much conversation with a dealer
from the State of New York, having serious intentions
of purchasing a horse to carry me to the banks of the
Mississippi, if one could have been got suitable for
the journey. The dealers attempted to palm colts on
me for aged horses, and seemed versed in all the

trickery which is practiced by their profession in
Britain.

A person showed me a model of a threshing-ma-
chine and a churn, for which he was taking orders,
and said he furnished the former at $30, or L.6, 1,0s.
sterling.   There were a number of French descend-
ants, who are engaged in the fur-trade, met in Chicago, for the purpose of settling accounts with the
Indians.   They were dressed in broadcloths and boots,
and boarded in the hotels.   They are a swarthy
scowling race, evidently tinged with Indian blood,
speaking the French and English languages fluently,
and much addicted to swearing and whisky.

The hotel at which our party was set down, was so
disagreeably crowded, that the landlord could not
positively promise beds, although he would do every-
thing in his power to accommodate us.   The house
was dirty in the extreme, and confusion reigned
throughout, which the extraordinary circumstances
of the village went far to extenuate.   I contrived,
however, to get on pretty well, having by this time
learned to serve myself in many things, carrying
water for washing, drying my shirt, wetted by the
rain of the preceding evening, and brushing my shoes.
The table was amply stored with substantial provisions, to which justice was done by the guests, although indifferently cooked, and still more so served
up.

When bed-time arrived, the landlord showed me
to an apartment about ten feet square, in which there

were two small beds already occupied, assigning me
in a corner a dirty pallet, which had evidently been
recently used, and was lying in a state of confusion.
Undressing for the night had become a simple proceeding, and consisted in throwing off shoes, neck-
cloth, coat and vest, the two latter being invariably
used to aid the pillow, and I had long dispensed with
a nightcap.   I was awakened from a sound sleep
towards morning, by an angry voice uttering horrid
imprecations, accompanied by a demand for the bed
I occupied.   A lighted candle, which the individual
held in his hand, showed him to be a French trader,
accompanied by a friend, and as I looked on them
for some time in silence, their audacity and brutality
of speech increased.   At length I lifted my head from
the pillow, leaned on my elbow, and with a steady
gaze, and the calmest tone of voice, said,—"Who are
you that address me in such language?"   The coun-
tenance of the angry individual fell, and he subduedly
asked to share my bed.   Wishing to put him to a
farther trial, I again replied,—"If you will ask the
favor in a proper manner, I shall give you an answer."
He was now either ashamed of himself, or felt his
pride hurt, and both left the room without uttering a
word.   Next morning, the individuals who slept in
the apartment with me, discovered that the intruders
had acted most improperly towards them, and the
most noisy of the two entered familarly into conversation with me during breakfast, without alluding to
the occurrence of the preceding evening.

LETTERS FROM A RAMBLER IN THE WEST

The following letters indicate certain aspects of the development of and the beauty of Illinois in 1837.

<u>Illinois in 1837</u>. Philadelphia: S. Augustus Mitchell and Grigg & Elliot, 1837

LETTERS FROM A RAMBLER IN THE WEST.

The six following letters from the pen of a talented young Philadelphian, a correspondent of the editor of the Pennsylvania Inquirer and Daily Courier, appeared in the columns of that gazette during the spring of the present year, under the title of "A Rambler in the West." They are beautifully written, and possess more than ordinary interest for those anxious to acquire information relative to the Western County, more particularly the state of Illinois.

No. I.

The Journey—The " Far West"—A Prairie on fire—Alton—Chicago.

Vandalia (Ill.), Jan. 29, 1837.

I promised you, my dear P——, when I left our good Quaker city, that I would give you some account of my wanderings. I had intended long ere this to have complied with my promise, but circumstances which we cannot control have hitherto prevented me from discharging that pleasing duty. I design now, however, to present you with a short account of my rambles.

The morning was cold and lowering, and the rain was descending in torrents, when the carriage arrived which was to convey me on my journey. It was truly a cheerless morn, and the streets through which we passed were almost deserted, save where here and there a single pedestrian, wrapping himself in his cloak, defied the "peltings of the pitiless storm." I need not say that the lowering appearance of the heavens tended in any degree to elevate the spirits of the youthful adventurer, who was leaving the scenes of his early days—the home of his youth—the thousand sweet associations of friends and "fatherland," on a tour of experiment to a new and almost unsettled country. But I had determined that the feelings of regret and despondency, so natural to the occasion, should not have a lodgement in my bosom—for experience had fully convinced me that they produce no beneficial results, but were oft-times productive of serious injury. Brushing away a hasty tear, which, in spite of all my philosophy, lingered in my eye, I bounded into the car with, apparently, a light and joyful heart. The door closed, and soon the last glimpse of my much-loved city faded from my view. After bestowing my hearty benedictions on it and the many kind friends its walls contained, I applied myself to the accomplishment of my purposes. I was anxious to obtain a knowledge of the country through which I passed, the character of its population, the nature of its soil and climate, and that mass of valuable information which travel alone can furnish.

My course lay through the line of internal improvements of the State of Pennsylvania, which are truly creditable to her citizens, and without much delay I arrived at Pittsburgh, whose business and activity indeed surprised me. I entered one of the noble steamers which crowded her wharves, and was soon proceeding at a rapid rate over the calm and tranquil waters of the "Beautiful River." Away we flew over its glad waters, and soon the spires and steeples of St. Louis peeped over the distant hills. I thought, upon my arrival there, that I was approaching the "far west;" but when I mentioned *west*, I was laughed at, and was pointed to that immense region which stretched far beyond the Mississippi, and was told, that when I travelled week after week, and thousands upon thousands of miles in that direction, I would then be approaching the confines of the "Great West." I was inclined to be discouraged; but being determined to visit the Illinois country, before attempting that arduous journey, I was soon on another boat, and ploughing the dark and troubled waters of the rapid Mississippi. The day I left St. Louis was peculiarly fine—one of those days in autumn when summer seems to linger on earth, as if unwilling to yield to Boreas' chill and nipping blast.

The scenery on the banks of the river was truly grand and sublime. Large jets of rock obtruded far into the stream, and reared their mighty heads almost to the clouds. So regular were they in their proportions, and so nicely chiselled, it seemed as if dame Nature had built for herself, in this western world, a huge and mighty castle, with lofty columns and frowning battlements, defying the skill of man to rival its majestic grandeur. Whilst enjoying the sublimity of the scene, night threw her mantle o'er the earth, and the "sentinel stars set their watch in the skies"—when suddenly the scene was lighted by a blaze of light illuminating every object around. Lo, it was the prairie on fire. Language cannot convey, words cannot express to you the faintest idea of the grandeur and splendour of that mighty conflagration. Methought that the pale queen of night, disdaining to take her accustomed place in the heavens, had despatched ten thousand messengers to light their torches at the altar of the setting sun, and that now they were speeding on the wings of the wind to their appointed stations. As I gazed on that mighty conflagration, my thoughts recurred to you, immured in the walls of a city, and I exclaimed, in the fullness of my heart,

> "Oh fly to the prairie, in wonder, and gaze
> As o'er the grass sweeps the magnificent blaze
> The world cannot boast so romantic a sight—
> A continent flaming 'mid oceans of light."

I arrived early on the following morning at Alton, which is a flourishing and thriving place, and presents a busy appearance. With its situation I was much pleased, but more gratified with the enterprize of its citizens. Every one here was active and industrious—there were no loungers—no idlers—no "loafers" to be seen. Every one seemed engaged in some occupation, and was pursuing it with industry and zeal. Large stores—as large as those which adorn our eastern cities —were building on the water's edge; dwelling houses of all sizes were springing up, and the hum of busy industry was sounding through the streets. I left this city with regret, being compelled to pursue my journey. After a very pleasant ride through a most delightful country, I arrived at Chicago.

Chicago is, without doubt, the greatest wonder in this wonderful country. Four years ago the savage Indian there built his little wigwam—the noble stag there saw undismayed his own image reflected from the polished mirror of the glassy lake—the adventurous settler then cultivated a small portion of those fertile prairies, and was living far, far away from the comforts of civilization. Four years have rolled by, and how changed that scene! That Indian is now driven far west of the Mississippi; he has left his native hills—his hunting grounds—the grave of his father—and now is building his home in the far west, again to be driven away by the mighty tide of emigration. That gallant stag no longer bounds secure o'er those mighty plains, but startles at the rustling of every leaf or sighing of every wind, fearing the rifles of the numerous Nimrods who now pursue the daring chase. That adventurous settler is now surrounded by luxury and refinement; a city with a population of over six thousand souls has now arisen; its spires glitter in the morning sun; its wharves are crowded by the vessels of trade; its streets are alive with the busy hum of commerce.

The wand of the magician or the spell of a talisman ne'er effected changes like these; nay, even Aladdin's lamp, in all its glory, never performed greater wonders. But the growth of the town, extraordinary as it is, bears no comparison with that of its commerce. In 1833, there were but four arrivals—or about 700 tons. In 1836, there were four hundred and fifty-six arrivals, or about 60,000 tons. Point me if you can to any place in this land whose trade has been increased in the like proportion. What has produced this great prosperity? I answer, its great natural advantages, and the untiring enterprize of its citizens. Its situation is unsurpassed by any in our land.

Lake Michigan opens to it the trade of the north and east, and the Illinois and Michigan canal, when completed, will open the trade of the south and south-west. But the great share of its prosperity is to be attributed to the enterprize of its citizens: most of them are young—many there are upon whose temple the golden lock of youth is not darkened; many who a short time since bade adieu to the fascinations of gay society, and immured themselves in the western wilderness, determining to acquire both fame and fortune. And what has been the result?— While many of their companions and former associates are now toiling and struggling in the lowly vale of life, with scarcely enough of the world's gear to drive away the cravings of actual want—the enterprizing adventurer has amassed a splendid fortune—has contributed to build up a noble city, the pride of his adopted state, and has truly caused the wilderness to bloom and blossom like the rose. Such are always the rewards of ever daring minds.

No. II.

Peru.

Peru, (Ill.) Feb. 4. 1837.

I resume my narrative.

The next point to which my attention was directed was Peru. This place will unquestionably become one of the greatest inland towns in the West, and second only to Chicago. A traveller riding through would smile if you were to tell him that this place was destined to become a city. One humble tenement is all it boasts, and a stranger would be apt to imagine, when you told him that a town was laid out there, and that lots were commanding from $1000 to $2500 apiece, that the speculating fever was raging with all-pervading influence. But upon careful examination and mature reflection, I have arrived at the conclusion above stated.

Peru is situated on the Illinois river, at the head of river navigation, and is the point of termination of the Illinois and Michigan Canal.

This canal, when completed, will be the most splendid project of internal improvement in the Union. Its dimensions are sixty feet wide at the top water line—36 feet wide at the bottom, and six feet deep—the estimated cost of which is nine millions. This is a great link in the grandest chain of internal improvements known in the world—"it unites the Mississippi with our inland seas, the Gulf of St. Lawrence with the Gulf of Mexico, and the Rocky mountains with the Atlantic coast." Where can be found a work of internal improvement more important than this?

Besides, the great central rail-road from the mouth of the Ohio terminates here. It is situated in the midst of a most fertile region, abounding in grain, in coal, in iron, and in hydraulic power. These things being considered, is it wrong to suppose that a large inland city will here arise? For myself I have no doubt of the fact, and would stake my reputation on the result. And but a few short months ago, the land there was entered by an enterprizing Pennsylvanian, (one who, by his business talents, enterprize, and unspotted reputation, has amassed a munificent fortune, and who can be pointed to as a distinguished example of the success which attends well-directed efforts) for a dollar and a quarter per acre—now it will readily command from 5000 to 10,000 dollars per acre.

I assure you, my dear ——, I have often wished as I was roaming over this beautiful country, that you were with me, to view this scene in all its glory, to cast your eyes over a boundless tract of land, on which stern Winter has cast his fleece-white mantle, to feel the west wind blowing on your cheek, and to experience that thrill of pleasure which the sight of those grand and mighty prairies alone can bestow. But perhaps you will see them at a more propitious period. Come, when Flora casts her garlands o'er the land,—Come,

> " When universal Pan
> Knit with the graces and the hours in dance,
> Leads on the gentle Spring."

Come, when the prairie flower is in blossom—come when " the rank grass is waving in billowy pride." Come when the chain that now binds these sluggish streams is loosed, and hear them laugh and merrily sing as they journey on to the ocean. Come then and view this rich, this growing, this flourishing country—examine its resources. See the field that is opened for enterprize and talent—look at the laurels which can be gained by exertion here, reflect on its increasing greatness, and the influence it is destined to exert upon our common country; and my word for it, a city life will lose its charms, and you will, without a sigh, bid it farewell, take up your staff, and come and pitch your tent in the great—the growing—the mighty—the boundless West.

No. III.

A Snow-Storm on the Prairie.

Peoria, (Ill.) Feb. 8, 1837.

> " Now sharp Boreas blows abroad, and brings
> The dreary winter on his frozen wings;
> Beneath the low-hung clouds, the sheets of snow
> Descend, and whiten all the fields below."

Such was the burden of my song when I awoke from a most refreshing slumber, and saw large white flakes descending, and the whole country covered with the snowy garb of winter. It is oft-times a very pleasant employment to watch the progress of a snow-storm, but then you must be sheltered from its violence, for I assure you, you cannot at all sentimentalize when you are breasting its fury, and have a long and dreary journey before you. However, this morning I was in a peculiarly good humour, and disregarding the solicitations of my friends, who begged me to remain until the storm had abated, I determined to resume my journey. Soon the merry jingle of the sleigh-bell announced to me that my vehicle was at the door of my friend's hospitable mansion—into it I sprung with joyous gaiety, and away we flew over the broad and boundless prairie. My noble steed seemed to feel a new excitement as he inhaled the fresh morning breeze, which lent life and vigour to every nerve.

A prairie is most beautiful in "the spring time of year," for then it is a garden formed and cultivated by nature's hand, where spring the clustering flowers which bloom in rich luxuriance, and "shed their fragrance on the desert air." But when stern winter casts her mantle over the earth, and binds the streams in icy fetters, then a prairie is a spectacle, grand and sublime, and will well repay for the hardships and privations of Western travelling. I was compelled, however, to ride against the wind, which whistled around and blew directly in my face. So violent was the storm that I was almost blinded by the thick flakes that were dashed directly in my eyes. Had I acted with prudence, I should have discontinued my journey, and made myself comfortable for the remainder of the day at the log hut where I dined—but I determined, in spite of wind and weather, to reach Peoria by night. Whilst progressing quietly on my way, gray twilight extended her evening shades on earth. Still I drove on, anxious to reach my point of destination. Not a single star peeped out from the heavens to shed its light on a benighted traveller. The storm increased in violence, and the cold winds whistled a wintry tune. I now found I had strayed from the road, and here was I on a broad prairie, without mark or mound, and had lost the trace, which was ere now covered by the falling snow.

Unfortunately I had left my compass behind, and now I was on a broad sea without a chart or compass, and without one stray light in the heavens whereby to direct my course. The mariner, when tossed upon the billows of the stormy ocean, has at least the satisfaction of knowing where he is, for the needle will always point to the pole, and his chart will tell him of the dangers in his path—but the weary traveller, who has lost his way on a Prairie, is on a boundless sea, where he cannot even tell the direction he is pursuing, for oft-times he will travel hour after hour, and still remain at nearly the same point from which he started. Had even one accommodating star beamed in the heavens, I should not have been the least disconcerted, for then I could have some object whereby to guide my steps. But all the elements combined against me, and I assure you my feelings were by no means comfortable. Memory ran over the sad history of the numerous travellers, who had been overtaken by night, and been buried in the falling snow; many who had started in the morning full of gay hopes and buoyant anticipations, who, ere another sun had risen, had found a cold and solitary grave—arrested in their course by the chill and icy hand of death. Alas, thought I, how true it is,

> "For them no more the blazing hearth shall burn—
> Or busy housewife ply her evening care;
> No children run to lisp their sire's return—
> Or climb his knee, the envied kiss to share."

Insensibly I felt a strong inclination to sleep—I had always heard that this was a dangerous symptom, and if I yielded to its influence, my life would certainly be lost. I endeavoured to shake off the drowsy feeling. Never before have I experienced such a strong inclination to sleep. Never before did I exert myself more to keep awake. I halloed—I shouted—I beat my breast to preserve animation, and tried every method to prevent my yielding to the drowsy influence. My noble horse was almost exhausted, and I myself began to despair of reaching a place of shelter—when suddenly a ray of light beamed upon the snow, and shed a shadow around me. Encouraged by this favourable token, I urged on. My jaded steed also seemed to know that he was approaching a place of shelter, for he quickened his pace, and shortly afterwards I discovered at a distance, a small log-hut, from whose window beamed a broad blaze of light. Soon was I at the door, and warmly welcomed by the kind owner, who shook the snow from my garments, and gave me a seat before a blazing fire.

Oh, how delightful was the sense of security as I sat sheltered from the wintry blast, and listened to the tales of the inmates, many of whom had, like me, been overtaken by the storm, and now were relating the events of their journey. I have passed many delightful evenings in the course of a short but eventful life—I have been at the festive board, where the wine-cup was pushed merrily around, and song, and laughter, and merriment abounded—I have mingled in the society of the gay—I have been

> " Where youth and pleasure meet
> To chase the glowing hours with flying feet."

But never have I passed a more happy evening than in the small and narrow cabin of that Illinois farmer.

No. IV.

Peoria—Illinois—The West.

Peoria, Feb. 8, 1837.

Early on the ensuing morning I arrived at Peoria. Peoria is situated on the Illinois river, and is in very truth a most beautiful site for a town. A few miles above, the river expands in a lake, upon the banks of which it is situated. The approach to the town is through alternate wood-land and prairie. It is the county-town of Peoria county, and has a bright prospect of rapidly increasing. It now has a population of fifteen hundred, and boasts of a large and commodious court-house and several fine mansions. It commands at all seasons an unbroken water communication with St. Louis, and is situated in a most delightful country. Its trade now is brisk, but it will increase in a ten-fold degree upon the completion of the Illinois and Michigan canal.

The highly respectable and talented author of " A Winter in the West," in one of his letters in 1834, expresses the following sentiments in reference to this work : " The State of Illinois, judging from the progress already made, will not complete the canal for half a century. The want of capital is here so great, as almost to seal up every outlet for enterprize, though they present themselves on every side, and our eastern capitalists are so completely ignorant of the prodigious resources of this region, that it will be long ere this defect will be supplied." To a part of this assertion we are obliged to enter our dissent, while to a part we will most cordially assent.

There exists no doubt on my mind, that this great and important work will be completed in five years; which, considering the immense magnitude of the under-taking, is certainly a short time. Every effort is now making to hasten its completion. A large part of it is under contract, and labourers are at work upon a considerable portion of the line. The Commissioners are men of acknowledged talent and integrity, and there is every reason to believe that the state, feeling a just and praiseworthy pride in the construction of this grand link in the chain of internal improvements, will urge its immediate completion. But we do agree with the author referred to, that our eastern capitalists are completely ignorant of the resources of this region.

Eastern capitalists cannot realize the great opportunities that every day present themselves for safe and profitable investment, and the great returns received for capital invested. With many the opinion is prevalent, that the accounts received through the medium of the press, are but the " puffs" of adventurous speculators, who by this method " crack up" their property, with the design of defrauding innocent purchasers. That this system has been most extensively pursued, cannot be denied; but that this country is destined to advance most rapidly in the scale of importance, and that investments judiciously made now, will insure a great profit, can be shown to the satisfaction of any reasoning mind.

Take out your map, and look at this noble state; look at its geographical situation, between 37 and 42 deg., N. lat. ; see the mighty Mississippi rolling its swift and turbid current along the western borders; look at the Wabash pursuing its silent way along the eastern side; see the " Beautiful River" washing the southern boundary; and look at that calm and placid stream, so properly denominated " a natural canal through a natural meadow," dividing the state and extending far and wide its fertilizing influence. What portion of our country is better watered or more capable of commanding a great hydraulic power? Reflect upon the face of the country and the nature of its soil. Here are no high and barren hills, or thick and dense woodlands, but broad and rolling prairies.

The state of Ohio will, at the next census, rank the third state in the confederacy; I mean as regards wealth and population—and yet what immense labour was required "to clear" a large portion of her territory, and then, at her early settlement, we had but a capital stock of six millions of souls. And if Ohio in thirty years rank as the third state in this Union, I ask what time will it require for a state to stand beside her—where the ground is already prepared by nature's hand for the farmer—when we have a capital stock of over thirteen millions, and when the facilities for emigration are ten-fold increased. Besides, Illinois contains a larger quantity of rich land than any other state, and therefore can maintain a large agricultural population, which is the great basis of national wealth. These things being considered, can we doubt that ere long these beautiful prairies will be adorned by the home of the settler—will re-echo the shrill whistle of the ploughman, as he "homeward plods his weary way," or the glad and joyous song of the reaper, as he gathers in the golden harvest?

Can we doubt that, ere long, Illinois will stand among her sister states—"her brow blooming with the wreath of science, her path strewed with the offerings of art, her temples rich in unrestricted piety," her prairies waving with the fruits of agriculture, her noble streams bearing upon their bosoms the produce of every clime, her borders filled with a rich and thriving population, attached to the institutions of our fathers; lovers of rational and enlightened liberty, and reflecting honour and glory upon our common country. But I must pause; my eyes grow heavy—my candle has almost burnt to its socket—and I must bid you good night. For now,

"The lamp of day is quench'd beneath the deep,
And soft approach the balmy hours of sleep."

No. V.

The East—The West—Enterprize—Agriculture.

Springfield, (Ill.) Feb. 27. 1837.

Here am I at the neat and pretty town of Springfield, a place of considerable trade, and containing a truly kind and hospitable population. The journey from Peoria to Springfield was most delightful. The air was pure and balmy—the heavens were blue—the roads were in fine order, and the "tout ensemble" was (to use a western term) "gorgeous." I am now snugly ensconced in a comfortable room, and intend to entertain you with a few detached and unconnected thoughts—and I will commence by saying, that the period of the year is fast approaching, when the tide of emigration rolls to the western world. As soon as the streams that now are bound by winter's chain, are loosed—as soon as the noble steamers, that "walk the waters like a thing of life," are plying up and down our rivers, the numbers of emigrants who will come to this land of promise, will far exceed that of any previous year. It is not merely the oppressed and afflicted of foreign climes, who have left their native hills for this land of peace and plenty; but many of our most enterprizing citizens, actuated, some, by a desire to improve their fortunes, and others by that truly American spirit—the love of rambling (for we are truly a migratory people,) will forsake their own comfortable homes, to examine the prospects of this much talked of, much written of, and far-famed country.

That those who possess sufficient intelligence, to appreciate and understand the advantages of this country, and a spirit of enterprize that will support them under the privations they must necessarily encounter, will be charmed and gratified with their western tour, I have no doubt; nor do I question that Illinois, in the progress of another year, will rank among her citizens, many of the most intelligent and enterprizing of our sister states. That this country possesses advantages of a most important character, and offers many attractions to the youthful adventurer—to him who would acquire both fame and fortune, can, I think, easily be shown, and I would present a few considerations tending to illustrate the subject.

And I will premise by saying, that there is no truth more evident to the reflecting mind, than that in this transatlantic world, every one must be the architect of his own fortune—no matter what course of life is adopted, be it professional or mechanical, the basis upon which every hope of future eminence must rest is, diligent, untiring, persevering application. Assuming this fact as granted, I would refer to the superiority of the western portion of our continent over the eastern, as regards the *acquisition of wealth—professional eminence—political distinction,* and the opportunity offered of *exercising influence on society* and *the destinies of our common country.*

As respects the acquisition of wealth—the great basis of all wealth is the agricultural interest, and that country must be the richest, which is the most capable of supporting the largest agricultural population. Land, rich and fertile soil, is the foundation of a nation's glory. It is true, that commerce tends much to enrich a people, and *large,* nay, *immense* fortunes, have been made in the pursuit of trade. But who does not know the mutations of trade!—who is not cognizant of the fluctuations of commerce! who is ignorant of the fact, that he who is engaged in commercial transactions may to-day be master of thousands, and roll in splendour and luxury, and to-morrow be a bankrupt, and know not where to lay his head? Do you seek for the evidence of this fact! Go to any of our large cities and inquire, and you will find the sad truth written in indelible characters, so plain that he who runs may read.

Now none of these mutations and fluctuations afflict the agricultural or producing class of society—no panics or pressures occur among them—a stormy sea cannot swallow up their earnings, nor a raging fire destroy the toil of years. The seed is dropped into the ground, and, "He who tempers the wind to the shorn lamb," sends the genial sunshine and refreshing showers, and the ripe and yellow harvest awaits the labourer's gathering.

Now, land in the western world is rich and fertile, and I will venture to say, that the soil of one of the prairies is more productive than any soil in your much loved state, not even excepting the far-famed Lancaster county, where the toil and labour of many years has been expended in improving it. This rich and fertile soil can be entered at $1.25 per acre, or bought "second-hand" for from $2.50 to $3.50 per acre. And it has been proved by actual experiment, that an enterprizing settler can break and sow 80 acres, and from the profits of his crop can realize a sufficient sum to enter and pay for his land; thus in one year, by the toil and labour of his hand, acquiring a fee-simple title to a fine and improving farm. In what portion of the eastern states can this be done! "I pause for a reply." Again—wealth will be acquired by *the natural increase* of the country.

This whole region (particularly the states of Illinois, Michigan, and Wisconsin Territory,) is filling up with great and unexampled rapidity. The increase of the country is truly wonderful, and one who has not witnessed it can scarcely believe it. The growth and prosperity of Chicago may be taken as a fair example of the unprecedented increase and advancement of the country. Cities and towns spring up in every quarter, and a mighty tide of emigration is rolling far and wide its fertilizing influence.

A small sum of money now judiciously invested, will increase in a ratio not even dreamed of by an eastern capitalist. Speak to them of the advantages of this region, and they smile, and tell you, you are exercising the powers of a fertile imagination. They manifest the same incredulity as was exhibited by the eastern monarch, when told by the philosopher, that he came from a country where water became congealed, and bore upon its bosom, men, and horses, and chariots. The monarch was indignant, that any one should attempt (as he supposed) to impose upon his good sense and experience; for he had been sunned in a burning clime, and there the streams were never bound by winter's chain, but were ever rolling their turbid waters, and yet the philosopher's tale was no less true than strange—and so it is with our eastern capitalists—they can form no idea of the increase and unexampled advancement of this country, for it is unparalleled in the annals of the world; and although they sometimes think they are very wise in discrediting our statements, they are only acting from a principle of human nature, (which is truly illiberal and narrow,) to disbelieve any thing that is contrary to their preconceived opinions, and has never occurred under the observation of their senses.

But judging of the future by the past, and can we have a better lamp to our steps than that of experience! what may we not anticipate from the increase of this country! It seems but yesterday that the whole valley of the Mississippi was a wilderness, untrodden, save by the moccasin of the red man, where the silence and solitude of nature was unbroken save by the shriek of the wolf, or the cry of the majestic eagle,

" As he gracefully wheel'd in the cloud-speckled sky."

Now, as if by work of enchantment, mighty states have there arisen, powerful in wealth and population—sisters of a common confederacy, and reflecting honour on our common country—cities and towns have sprung up like stars above the horizon, and the whole scene is alive with the industry and enterprize of man. Why, I ask, will not land in Illinois be as valuable as in any portion of the Atlantic states! Why will not land along the borders of the Illinois and Michigan canal command as high a price as that upon the Erie canal! The soil is far more productive, requires less toil to prepare for the hand of the farmer, and the market for produce is far superior to any in the east. Does any one pretend to say that lands in any portion of the west will ten years hence be sold for $1.25 per acre! if so, he arrives at that conclusion by a process of reasoning which I cannot understand. To the mechanic—to the labourer—to the working classes of society, this fact offers great encouragement; for here they can earn large wages, and the small sums which they invest will increase most rapidly.

Again, wealth depends upon *economy*. It is the prudent, saving man, and not the prodigal, who acquires a fortune;—a penny saved is a penny earned, was the maxim of a wise philosopher, and its truth has been fully tested. Now, in a new country, fewer temptations are in your path—fewer opportunities for wasting and squandering the wealth earned by your labour—fewer inducements are presented for the exhibition of extravagances and prodigality, than in our large eastern cities, where luxury is the reigning vice—where man strives as the object of his highest ambition, to outrival his fellow man in the magnificence of his equipage, the extravagance of his table, and the brilliancy of his entertainments.

These considerations, then, the low price of rich and fertile soil, the certain and great increase of the country, and the want of opportunities for the display of extravagance and prodigality, exhibit, in a faint degree, the superiority of the western country—the young and rising west—over the over-populated and already exhausted east. If then wealth be the object of pursuit—if the acquirement of a fortune be the "ultima thule" of your wishes, here is the field upon which to commence your efforts—a field already ripe with the golden harvest, and only waiting the labourer's gathering.

No VI.

The Acquisition of Wealth—Young Men and Old—Advantages of the West.

Jacksonville, March 3, 1837.

In my last, I endeavoured to exhibit the superiority of the Western Country over the eastern, as regards the acquisition of wealth. Unfortunately for us, the desire for wealth is the ruling passion of our nation—a passion developed in early life, sanctioned by parental admonition, and strengthened by each advancing year—almost the first principle instilled into the youthful mind, is the importance of wealth, and almost the first object to which the youthful energies are directed, is the acquisition of a fortune. We will not stop to show the pernicious influence which this universal worship at the shrine of Marnmon has upon the morals, the literary taste, and the intellectual greatness of our people. We will not stop to exhibit the dangerous tendency of this money-making spirit, to destroy those nice distinctions between right and wrong—to vitiate the public taste—to impair the force of native intellect, and to delay the glorious triumphs of the mind.

This fact we will leave to an abler pen, confident that our feeble efforts would be of little avail in checking that ardent and earnest desire for wealth so prevalent through the land. But there are those to whom, in speaking of the advantages of a new country, we can point to higher and nobler inducements than the mere acquisition of worldly goods—many who are engaged in the noble employment of cultivating and improving the human intellect, and desire a broad and ample field upon which to exert the energies of that immortal mind with which Providence has blessed them.

To those we would speak in the language of affectionate regard, and would endeavour to convince them that, if they desire distinction in that branch of science to which their attention has been directed—if eminence in their profession is the object of their wishes, that they have only to summon up moral courage to enter boldly on a scene of action which will inevitably lead to happy and glorious results. But they must be endued with the spirit of lofty determination and noble resolution—a determination that will brave all obstacles—a resolution that will support them under all privations—not that weak and sickly resolution that every difficulty discourages, and every obstacle disheartens; but that bold and manly resolution which, fixing its eagle eye upon the topmost height, determines to reach the destined mark, and, like the thunder-bearer of Jove, when storms and tempests beat around, soar higher and loftier, and sustains itself by the force and sublimity of its own elevation.

Among the number of advantages which the West has over the East, may be enumerated the following:—

1. In the East, the professions are monopolized by the older members—in the WEST, the responsible duties of the professions are confided to the young men.

2. In the West, greater inducements for the acquisition of a fortune being held out by the farming or agricultural interest, and great privations having necessarily to be encountered, the number of professional men is FEWER than at the East, and consequently the field is more ample.

3. In a new country, every thing being to build up and construct, greater opportunity is offered for the exercise of professional talent.

4. The tendency of a new country being to develope and bring forward youthful talent, exerts a highly favourable influence upon boldness, force, and originality of intellect.

In illustration of the first proposition, we need but appeal to the experience of every young professional man. How few, how very few, even of our most active and intelligent young men can, in our large eastern cities, earn a respectable livelihood! One or two of the most eminent and experienced monopolize the most important and lucrative portions of the business. The community look up to them with confidence, for they believe their minds are matured by wisdom and ripened by experience, and the young men are permitted to remain in almost total inactivity.

Here and there an instance may occur of a young man of high and noble endowments entering boldly into the arena, and, by the force of his intellect and the brilliancy of his talents, commanding a large share of public patronage; but for one who thus happily has burst the fetters which confine and restrain the youthful intellect, how many have toiled and struggled in the lowly vale of life, then "dropped into the tomb, unhonoured and unknown!"—The aged and experienced will not confide their business to youthful heads, for they cannot realize that those whom a few short years ago they dandled on the knee, or saw engaged in the simple and artless amusements of early childhood, are prepared to discharge the high and responsible duties appertaining to a profession.

Now, in the West the population is mostly young, consisting chiefly of youthful adventurers, who have left their peaceful homes with the determination to reap the advantages of a new country. A young professional man has enlisted in his behalf, not the cold and sordid influence of those whose feelings have been chilled by a contact with a selfish world, but the warm and glowing feelings of early youth. He is there surrounded not by the aged fathers of the profession—those whose brows are silvered o'er by the frosts of time—not the experienced soldiers who have conquered o'er and o'er again in the fight, and advance to the contest confident of success; but he beholds himself surrounded by his equals—his companions and associates, each striving to gain the prize of public approbation—each struggling to win the pure and spotless laurels which will crown the victor's brow.

In illustration of the second proposition, we can only add, that there can be no doubt that if the acquisition of wealth be the object of pursuit, greater inducements are held out by the farming and agricultural interest. A professional life is at all times a life of toil, and he who aspires to its highest honours must remember that they are only to be attained by untiring unremitting effort. The pecuniary emoluments are small compared with other occupations of life, and he who desires professional eminence must not expect to reap the same amount of this world's good as he whose soul is engaged in the pursuit of trade.

Now an enterprising emigrant, when he leaves his native village, as he turns to take the last lingering look of the home of his affections—as he beholds the spire of the village church, where so oft he has worshipped the God of his fathers, glittering in the morning sun, the last wish which animates his bosom, is the hope of some not far distant day, returning to the scenes of his childhood, where every object brings some sweet association, laden with the fruits of his toil. In fine, it is wealth that he hopes to attain, and it is the prospect of reaping golden fruits which enables him manfully to endure the privations to which he is subjected. He arrives at the land of promise, and examines the prospect of improving his fortune which the country affords. He finds that the tiller of the soil is the one who reaps the most productive harvest, and no matter what profession he may have adopted,—no matter what branch of science may have hitherto occupied his attention—he relinquishes its pursuit—forgets the obligations his profession imposes on him, and forsakes his calling to assume the manly and independent, but at the same time more profitable employment of the farmer.

But few, few alas! of professional men of the proper stamp and character emigrate to a new country. It is the hardy yeoman and independent mechanic who has the moral courage to emigrate to a new but growing country. The young professional man is unfortunately too attached to the comforts of a city life. He loves his ease too much to think of forsaking the attractions and fascinations which have thrown their spells around him, and he will content himself with wasting and squandering the precious hours of youth, (which are truly the wealth of future remembrance,) in the pursuit of the phantom pleasure, which will forever, like Creusa's ghost, fly from his embrace. In the East the professions are over-stocked, and it is indeed distressing in our large eastern cities to see the large number of professional young men, without any employment to occupy their time—frittering away the powers of their intellect, and acquiring habits that will inevitably tend to prevent attaining either standing or eminence in their profession—when if they would only listen to the voice of reason, and obey its dictates, they might have the certain prospect of advancing the character of their profession—being useful to society—exercising influence on our country, and building up a name

> "That long shall hallow every space,
> And be each purer soul's high resting place."

But I find if I continue the subject now, I shall be obliged to trespass on your limits. Adieu.

RAMBLER.

THE END.

BASIC FACTS

Capital: Springfield.
Largest City: Chicago
Nicknames: Prairie State; Sucker State.
Song: "Illinois."
Abbreviation: IL

21st State to enter Union, Dec. 3, 1818.
Area: 56,400 sq. mi.
Population (1970 Census): 11,128,000.

State Tree: Native Oak.

State Bird: Cardinal.

State Flower: Native Violet.

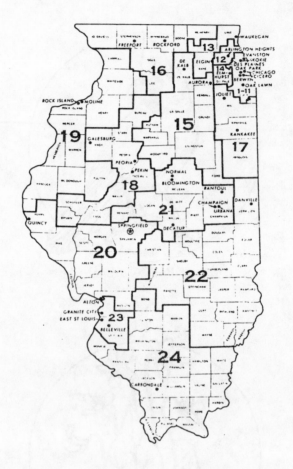

Congressional Districts of Illinois

SELECTED BIBLIOGRAPHY

Alvord, Clarence Walworth, ed. The Critical Period,
    1763-1765. Springfield, Ill.: The Trustees of the
    Illinois State Historical Library, 1915.

_____. The Illinois Country, 1673-1818. Springfield:
    Published by the Illinois Cenyennial Commission,
    1920.

_____. Illinois in the 18th Century. Springfield:
    Illinois State Journal Co., State Printers, 1905.

_____ and Clarence Edwin Carter. The New Regime, 1765-
    1767. Springfield, Ill.: Illinois State Historical
    Library, 1916.

Angle, Paul McClelland. Prairie State: Impressions of
    Illinois, 1673-1967 by Travelers. Chicago: Univer-
    sity of Illinois Press, 1968.

_____ and Richard L. Beyer. Handbook of Illinois His-
    tory. Springfield, Ill.: The Illinois State Histor-
    ical Society, 1943

Bateman, Newton and P. Selby, eds. Historical Encyclo-
    pedia of Illinois. 2 vols. Chicago: Munsell Pub-
    lishing Company, 1933.

Boggess, Arthur Clinton. The Settlement of Illinois,
    1778-1830. Chicago: The Historical Society, 1908.

Bogue, Allan G. From Prairie to Corn Belt: Farming on
    Illinois and Iowa Prairies in the Nineteenth Century.
    Chicago: University of Chicago Press, 1963.

Carter, Clarence Edwin. Great Britain and the Illinois
    Country, 1763-1774. Washington: The American His-
    torical Association, 1910.

Church, Harry Victor. Illinois. Boston and New York:
    D. C. Heath and Company, 1931.

Conger, John Leonard and W. E. Hall, eds. History of
    the Illinois River Valley. 3 vols. Chicago: The
    S. J. Clarke Publishing Co., 1932.

Dunne, Edward Fitzsimons. Illinois, The Heart of the
    Nation. 3 vols. Chicago and New York: The Lewis
    Publishing Company, 1933.

Gray, James. The Illinois. New York: Farrar and Rine-
    hart, Incorporated, 1940.

Humphrey, Grace. Illinois, The Story of the Prairie

State. Indianapolis: The Bobbs-Merrill Company,
1917.

Johnson, Charles Beneulyn. <u>Illinois in the Fifties; Or
a Decade of Development, 1851-1860</u>. Champaign, Ill.:
Flanigan-Peason Co., 1918.

Jones, Lottie E. <u>Decisive Dates in Illinois History</u>.
Danville, Ill.: Illinois Printing Company, 1909.

Kallenbach, Joseph E. and Jessamine S. Kallenbach.
<u>American State Governors, 1776-1976</u>. 3 vols. Dobbs
Ferry, N. Y.: Oceana Publications, Inc., 1977-

Mather, Irwin F. <u>The Making of Illinois</u>. Chicago: A.
Flanagan Company, 1935.

Maue, August. <u>History of Illinois</u>. New York and Chicago: C. Scribner's Sons, 1927.

Monaghan, James. <u>This Is Illinois: Pictorial History</u>.
Chicago: University of Chicago Press, 1949.

Pease, Theodore Calvin. <u>The Frontier State, 1818-1848</u>.
Springfield, Ill.: Illinois Centennial Commission,
1918

_____. <u>The Story of Illinois</u>. 3rd rev. ed. by Marguerita
J. Pease. Chicago University Press, 1965.

Pooley, William Vipond. <u>The Settlement of Illinois from
1830 to 1850</u>. Madison, Wis., 1908.

Robinson, Luther Emerson and Irving Moore. <u>History of
Illinois</u>. New York and Cincinnati: American Book
Company, 1926.

Smith, George Washington. <u>History of Illinois and Her
People</u>. 6 vols. Chicago and N. Y.: The American
Historical Society, Inc., 1927.

Steiner, Gilbert Yale and Samuel K. Gove. <u>Legislative
Politics in Illinois</u>. Urbana: University of Illinois Press, 1960.

Tingley, Donald F., ed. <u>Essays in Illinois History in
Honor of Glenn Huron Seymour</u>. Carbondale: Southern
Illinois University Press, 1968.

NAME INDEX